Begonias

Mike Stevens

FIREFLY BOOKS

Dedication

I wish to dedicate this book to my wife, Isobel. Not only has she given ongoing support to my begonia involvements over the years, but also, without her many hours of assistance with this specific project, this book would not have been written.

Acknowledgments

I would like to thank my many fellow "Begoniacs" throughout the world for sharing their experiences with me over the years. These growers are too numerous to name individually, but in many respects this is their book as much as mine—I have been the midwife! Thanks are also due to the begonia lovers who have allowed me to photograph their plants and gardens. I am also indebted to growers who supplied slides from which a few were selected to fill gaps in my collection. A final thanks to my editors, Pamela McGeorge and Tracey Borgfeldt.

Page 1: A lovely example of a cream-red picotee.

Page 2: A container-grown standard with a beautiful head of flowers.

Page 3: A vibrant yellow flower with classic rose-form blooms.

A FIREFLY BOOK

Published by Firefly Books Ltd. 2002

First Printing

National Library of Canada Cataloguing in Publication Data

Stevens, Mike, 1942-
    Begonias
Includes index.
ISBN 1-55297-552-5 (bound) ISBN 1-55297-551-7 (pbk.)
1. Begonias. I. Title.
SB413.B4S84 2002 635.9'33627 C2001-901800-2

U.S. Cataloging-in-Publication Data
(Library of Congress Standards)

Stevens, Mike, 1942-
    Begonias / Mike Stevens. –1st ed.
[96] p. : col. photos. ; cm.
Includes index.
Summary: Guide to using and growing begonias in your garden. Includes design ideas, sources and directory of begonias.
ISBN 1-55297-552-5 ISBN 1-55297-551-7 (pbk.)
1. Begonias. I. Title.
635.933627 21 CIP SB413.B4.574 2002

Published in Canada in 2002 by Firefly Books Ltd., 3680 Victoria Park Avenue, Willowdale, Ontario M2H 3K1

Published in the United States in 2002 by Firefly Books (U.S.) Inc., P.O. Box 1338, Ellicott Station, Buffalo, New York 14205

Cover design Shelley Watson, Sublime Design; Design Errol McLeary; Typesetting Jazz Graphics, Auckland; Printed in Hong Kong through Colorcraft Ltd

Contents

Introduction

It was love at first sight when I first saw Large-flowered tuberous begonias growing at a specialist begonia nursery. The vibrant range of colors and the luminosity of the mass display held me spellbound. I was also taken by the fact that begonias, unlike many other plants, have a very long flowering season of up to four months or longer.

My first attempts to grow these begonias proved to be disastrous, and I was unable to source much information to assist me. It was then I discovered and joined a local group of begonia enthusiasts and began to learn the tricks of the trade. I gradually absorbed information from this group and from my mentor, Ken Mackey, who was then president of the group. I learned there were many other types of begonias, equally wonderful in their own way.

By listening to other growers with the "Begonia Disease", it was obvious that, like myself, they were disadvantaged by a lack of a good local source of current information, particularly in relation to tuberous begonias. It was at this point that the magazine *Begonia News* was launched under my editorship. This bimonthly magazine featured letters and articles by both experienced and novice growers, and now has an international readership. The next step was to set up a web site, linked to those of similar enthusiasts in many other countries, to foster interest in begonias and supply the much-needed information.

My aim in this book has been to keep things simple, practical, and informative. Although some mention is made of all groups of begonias, tuberous begonias are the main focus. In some countries, these plants are frequently grown for exhibition and competition, requiring special techniques, such as limiting a plant to one bloom. However, as this is not the case everywhere, I describe the general culture that applies to the average home gardener.

To ensure the information in this book covers a range of conditions, I have consulted with experienced growers across both the United States and Canada. These people, a number of whom have been contributors to *Begonia News*, grow begonias in very cold zones to areas of considerable heat. In particular, I would like to acknowledge the contribution of Lyn Aegard of the Master Gardeners of Thunder Bay, and Avery Wagg, the webmaster of the Canadian Begonia Society web page for so generously sharing their knowledge of cold-climate culture.

Beware the Begonia Disease. It can be addictive, and my wife describes it as terminal. Once hooked, there is no cure, so, fellow "Begoniacs", enjoy your plants!

A field of begonias in Belgium, the world's largest producer of begonia tubers.

Hardiness Zone Map

This map has been prepared to agree with a system of plant hardiness zones that have been accepted as an international standard and range from 1 to 11. It shows the minimum winter temperatures that can be expected on average in different regions.

In this book, where a zone number has been given, the number corresponds with a zone shown here. That number indicates the coldest areas in which the particular plant is likely to survive through an average winter.

Note that these are not necessarily the areas in which it will grow best. Because the zone number refers to the minimum temperatures, a plant given zone 7, for example, will obviously grow perfectly well in zone 8, but not in zone 6. Plants grown in a zone considerably higher than the zone with the minimum winter temperature in which they will survive might well grow but they are likely to behave differently. Note also that some readers may find the numbers a little conservative; we felt it best to err on the side of caution.

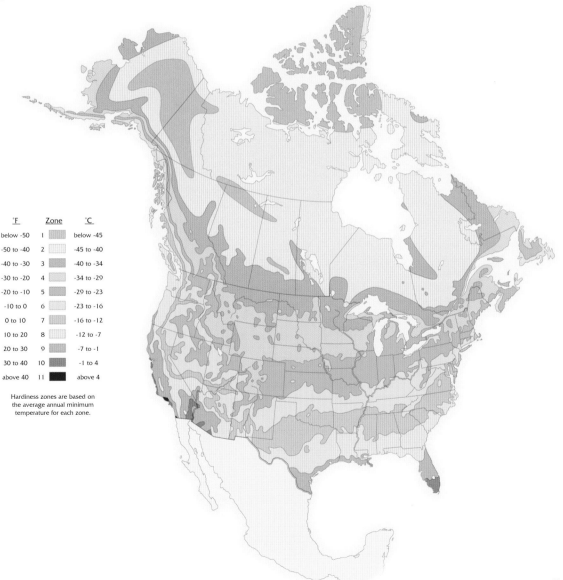

°F	Zone	°C
below -50	1	below -45
-50 to -40	2	-45 to -40
-40 to -30	3	-40 to -34
-30 to -20	4	-34 to -29
-20 to -10	5	-29 to -23
-10 to 0	6	-23 to -16
0 to 10	7	-16 to -12
10 to 20	8	-12 to -7
20 to 30	9	-7 to -1
30 to 40	10	-1 to 4
above 40	11	above 4

Hardiness zones are based on the average annual minimum temperature for each zone.

CHAPTER 1

History and Key Discoveries

It may come as a surprise to many to find that the begonia family, Begoniaceae, is so diverse, for it is thought to have as many as 1000 known and identified species, plus countless hundreds of hybrids of various types.

In their natural environment, begonias grow in rain forests and in the tropical and subtropical regions of the world, often at high altitudes. They are found on all continents, with the exception of Europe and Australia.

The majority of all begonias fall into the succulent category and are therefore susceptible to frosts in cooler regions, but this does not preclude them from being grown in these areas with suitable protection, overwintering, or as annuals.

As a generalization, begonias are grouped into three main categories according to their root structure, namely fibrous, rhizomatous, and tuberous or bulbous. However, the American writers Mildred and Edward Thompson, in their authoritative book *Begonias, The Complete Reference Guide* (now out of print), divided the genus into eight horticultural classifications. These have been adopted in this book as a convenient grouping when describing the characteristics and culture of begonias in more detail.

Botanical terms

Genus is the name given to plants united by distinct common characteristics, e.g., the genus *Begonia*. A genus is a member of a still larger botanical grouping called a family, and for begonias this is the Bego-

Begonia Tuberhybrida 'Amy'

niaceae. Within each genus are many species. Individual plants of a species are alike and can breed with each other, breeding true from seed, although they can also be propagated from cuttings.

The species name follows immediately after the name of the genus to which it belongs, e.g., *Begonia sutherlandii*, or in the abbreviated form *B. sutherlandii*, where the genus is begonia and the species is sutherlandii. The name of a species is always written in lower case letters, never capitals, and the genus and these words are usually set in italics. A smaller subdivision within a species is a subspecies, indicated in its name by the letters ssp., e.g., *B. grandis* ssp. *evansiania*, and yet another small subdivision, exemplified in the name *B. cucullata* var *hookeri*, indicates that this is a variety that differs slightly in its botanical structure.

Opposite: *Begonia pearcei*

A hybrid is a plant derived from the interbreeding or cross-fertilization of two different species or their variants. This may be the result of either intentional or accidental crossing. A hybrid specifically cultivated for horticultural or garden purposes is known as a cultivar or variety. Most hybrids or cultivars have to be reproduced by vegetative methods such as cuttings (cloning), as their seeds do not come true, and a good number of these plants are, in fact, sterile.

The correct way to record the name of a hybrid or cultivar is with the first letter of the name in capitals and the whole name in single inverted commas: *Begonia* 'Amy' or *B.* 'Amy'.

Another term used in this book is Tuberhybrida, meaning a hybrid of a tuberous variety. This differentiates it from *Begonia sutherlandii*, which, although tuberous, is, in fact, a species begonia. Thus the full name of the above example is *Begonia* Tuberhybrida 'Amy'. (In books written before a revision of the International Code of Nomenclature in 1995, 'x' would be used before the hybrid name to designate a cross: *Begonia* x Tuberhybrida 'Amy'.)

Origins

Quite some years before botanical classifications for begonias were formally established, historical documents show that the genus later known as *Begonia* had been discovered and classified under different names. One of these early finds was a plant which, although discovered in Mexico before 1577 by one Father Francisco Hernandez, was known only after 1651, when its description appeared in a book published posthumously. This plant, a tuberous species, was given the name *totoncaxoxo coyollin* (subsequently identified as *B. gracilis*). However, even as early as the 14th century, Chinese writings describe a plant now identified as *B. grandis* Dryander.

In 1690, Charles Plumier, a Franciscan Monk and botanist, discovered six plants in the West Indies, none of which fitted into any genus known at that time. The descriptions and botanical draw-

Above: A display of tuberous begonias in a public conservatory.
Opposite: The striking patterns of a Rex Cultorum leaf.

ings allowed their identification as a totally new genus, which Plumier then dedicated to his patron, Michel Begon, hence the genus name, *Begonia*. Begon, who had a strong interest in botany, was at that time Governor (Intendant) of Haiti.

Four key discoveries

Since that time, many species have been discovered, and discoveries continue to this day. It was, however, in the latter part of the 19th century that four separate finds led to a big rise of interest in begonias among horticulturists and collectors. This led in turn to the development of hybrids of the four more popular groups of begonias grown today.

1. The Rex ancestors

In England in 1856, there was a chance discovery among some imported orchids from Assam, India, of a begonia with amazing leaf patterns. This new species was quickly recognized and given the name

Begonia rex Putzey, *Rex* meaning "king" in Latin. The potential for commercial development because of the stunning leaves led to much hybridization, giving us what is known today as the Rex Cultorum group.

2. Bedding begonias' origins

Another major discovery occurred in 1821, again by chance, when the species *Begonia semperflorens* (*B. cucullata* var *hookeri*) was found in some soil around plants brought out of Brazil to the Berlin Botanic Gardens. Its commercial potential was only recognized in the late 1870s, when it was crossed with a recently discovered species, *B. schmidtiana*. This produced the beginnings of the Semperflorens group, also popularly known as Wax or Bedding begonias.

3. Winter houseplants

The potential for the development of winter-flowering begonias was recognized following the discovery in 1880 of one such, *Begonia socotrana*, by Issac Balfour on the island of Socotra in the Indian Ocean. This, the only begonia species in the bulbous class, was crossed with summer-flowering tuberous types. The result was a winter-flowering begonia with tuberous characteristics, the name Hiemalis being adopted for the group in 1933. The Rieger strain, developed by Otto Rieger in 1955, is more floriferous and resistant to mildew. Progress continues with the development of more hybrids in this popular group.

Other crosses of *Begonia socotrana*, this time with another winter-flowering tuberous species, *B. dregei*, resulted in the formation of a floriferous, winter-flowering group, later named Cheimantha and sometimes known as Christmas or Lorraine begonias. *B. dregei* was one of the oldest begonias in cultivation, having been imported into Europe about 1836 from South Africa. It had pure white flowers, which later assisted greatly in the breeding of better whites.

11

4. Tuberhybrida

In contrast to the rather accidental discoveries detailed above, professional plant collectors sent out by nurseries found the ancestors of tuberous begonias. The plants were sent back to Europe, where nurserymen began propagation and hybridization to satisfy the growing desire of Victorians for anything new.

About 1850, Henderson's nursery introduced *Begonia cinnabarina*, discovered in Bolivia. It has small orange flowers displayed on tall erect stems, and large leaves.

In the 1860s, a number of tuberous species were found high in the forests of Bolivia and Peru, in the Andes of South America. Of these plants, the following four were discovered by Richard Pearce, who worked for the Chelsea firm of James Veitch & Son.

Begonia boliviensis was discovered in Bolivia. It has long slender stems with narrow scarlet flowers and was a major influence in the breeding of today's Pendula begonias.

Begonia pearcei was also discovered in Bolivia and is very compact. Like *B. boliviensis*, it is still grown today. It has wonderful, dark green leaves with a velvet texture and very marked veins. The small, bright yellow flowers add interest, as it is the only yellow among the tuberous species. Its introduction into the breeding programs led to today's yellows.

Begonia veitchii, collected in Peru, is another compact plant. The flowers are bright red-orange. They have rounded petals and are displayed on strong erect stalks well above the foliage. Both these characteristics have been passed on to modern hybrids. This variety is still grown by collectors.

Begonia rosiflora (or *B. rosaeflora* according to some authorities) comes from Peru and has small pink flowers, although a later sport or mutation produced white blooms, helpful in developing white varieties. Nowadays, this species is generally considered to be the same as *B. veitchii*, since the two forms differ only slightly, the main difference being in flower color.

Above: *Begonia* 'Lady Rowena', a recent Blackmore & Langdon introduction.
Below: The flowers of *Begonia boliviensis*.

Above: A ruffled basket from Antonelli Brothers of California. This area is the largest producer of tubers in the USA.

Another collector for Veitch's was Walter Davis, who discovered *Begonia davisii* in 1876, also in Peru. This is a small compact species with hairy, bluish green leaves and orange flowers with contrasting yellow stamens. It was used in the breeding of many of today's Multiflora types due to its extreme dwarf nature.

From these species, with the addition of one or two other minor ones, have come the tuberous begonias we know today—the Large-flowered types, Pendulas, Multifloras, Non-stops, and the now less popular Fimbriata, Marmorata, and Crispa types.

The bulk of the development was done in the 20th century in both Europe and North America. Since World War I, the firm of Blackmore & Langdon, which was established in England in 1901 and still operates to this day, has done most of the work breeding the Large-flowered named varieties. In the United States, the firm of Vetterle & Reinelt was established in the mid-1930s and set about·their breeding program. Under the guiding hand of Frank Reinelt, this saw the introduction for the first time of the Ruffled types. Reinelt was also successful in perfecting the rose form bloom in the Large-flowered type. Although they did name a few varieties, their main business was in selling good-quality tubers.

In more recent years, this work has been continued by the Antonelli Brothers of California, who have also introduced an excellent range of frilled basket types. The Brown Bulb Co. also contributed a great deal to the development of improved strains of tuberous begonias in North America; the "Santa" series was introduced by them in the late 1940s. As with other parts of the world, keen amateurs in both the United States and Canada hybridize quality blooms, many of which are registered with the American Begonia Society.

In Europe, particularly in France, Belgium, and Germany, the emphasis was mainly on improving the smaller-flowered Multiflora types, which were very popular. Many were produced and named in the latter part of the 19th century, when much work was done to produce varieties that would come true from seed. The firm of Benary in Germany was very successful in both these fields and is a major supplier of seed today.

CHAPTER 2

Culture of Non-tuberous Begonias

All non-tuberous begonias are frost-tender. The ideal climate for outdoor culture is zone 10 and warmer, but they will also grow in sheltered garden situations in zone 9. For optimal growth, temperatures between 54° F (12°C) and 76°F (24°C) are required. Although they like good ventilation (which helps prevent mildew), they do not like cold winds. Fortunately, there are many that grow well indoors and some that are suited to container culture only, so even growers in cooler areas can enjoy these plants year-round as houseplants, and in conservatories or terrariums.

Wherever they are grown, good light is essential. Morning and afternoon sun will help give good foliage color, prevent legginess, and improve the quality and quantity of the flowers. For best results avoid dark corners.

Humid conditions of around 40–60 percent are ideal. In the house as container plants, the humidity can be increased by setting the container over, but not in, water, e.g., by placing the pot on some pebbles in a saucer. This is particularly useful in the winter if the heating system is drying out the atmosphere.

All begonias prefer free-draining soil and, if grown in containers, a free-draining open mix. Beware of over-watering container-grown plants. Water should be given only when the mix is dry to the touch, but then it is important to add enough water to thoroughly moisten the mix. Care should be taken, however, to avoid watering the leaves.

Opposite: *Begonia* 'Orange Rubra', a low-growing, cane-like hybrid that flowers indoors year-round.

Above: *Begonia cucullata* (semperflorens species) on left and *Begonia holtonis* (shrub-like) on right, grown outside in zone 10.

Every few weeks during the growing season, a weak liquid fertilizer may be applied, but only when the mix is damp, or the roots will burn. Such applications should cease during the dormant period (winter).

Pinching out improves branching and bushiness, and pruning improves the shape. Damaged or aging leaves and spent flowers should be removed.

In general, these plants are remarkably free of disease. Attention to the above requirements will go a long way toward preventing mildew, the main problem that can occur.

Non-tuberous begonias by type

Since this book is primarily a guide to culture rather than to the identification of individual plants, I

15

Begonia albopicta, the "Guinea-wing begonia", a cane-like species with typical angel-wing, silver-spotted leaves.

have chosen from each group a few examples that are more readily available, or that I have particularly enjoyed growing. All are suitable for container culture and may be grown as houseplants.

1. Cane-like

Today, over 200 species and cultivars are known in this group, so named because of their stiff cane-like stems. Many of the Cane-like species grown nowadays originated in Brazil, with most of the plants in this group having been discovered in the 19th century. They are deservedly popular for their graceful, pendulous clusters of flowers, which last for long periods in the warmer areas, and range in color from white through pink to salmon-orange. The leaves, which vary considerably in shape, often have attractive silver or white dots and markings.

Plants can vary in size from a mere 12 in (30 cm) tall to in excess of 15 ft (4.6 m) high when grown

outdoors in warmer climates. The Superba types are the tallest growing and generally have spotted leaves, while the Mallet types are squatter, not growing much above 24 in (60 cm). These mostly have lovely mahogany-red foliage covered in red hairs. In addition, there are many other types generally grouped under the description of low-, medium- and tall-growing. A number are popularly known as "Angel Wing" begonias, and others as "Tree" begonias.

Canes do well in both containers and open ground but, as these plants are deep-rooted, containers should be large enough to accommodate a fairly large root system. Repotting from time to time is desirable, particularly in spring.

Propagation by cuttings is relatively easy, and the best results will be achieved using tip cuttings taken from growing shoots. These should be cut to a length that includes three nodes, cutting just below the lower node. Leaves are stripped from the bottom of the stem, leaving only two or three, and the lower portion of the stem is inserted into the rooting medium. Roots will appear in three to four weeks. Leaf cuttings are not recommended.

2. Shrub-like

The second largest begonia group is the Shrub-like, which now numbers about 300 species and hybrids. Apart from a small number that have their origin in Asia and Africa, Central and South America were the source. As early as 1688 in Jamaica, the physician and naturalist Hans Sloane discovered *Begonia acutifolia*, which is still grown today. (It is noteworthy that Sloane's discoveries inspired Plumier, the originator of the genus *Begonia*, to travel to this area.)

Plants in this group have woody stems and excellent foliage, which ranges from being extremely hairy to totally bare. Leaves are quite varied in shape, size, and texture. The plants flower really well if a good general fertilizer is applied regularly. Flower colors are generally in the range of white, cream or pink, although a few are available in other shades such as yellow and salmon. As their

name would suggest, they tend to be bushy plants, producing shoots at the base. They often have dense growth and make good container specimens.

When grown outdoors, the bare-leaved varieties are able to tolerate more direct sunlight than their hairy counterparts, due to the reflective nature of the leaf surface.

Above left: *Begonia serratipetala*, a shrub-like species with upright stems and distinctive foliage.
Above right: *Begonia cubensis*, "Holly-leaf begonia", a shrub-like species with bushy growth, many stems and ever-blooming, white flowers.

The preferred method of propagation is by taking cuttings, using the tips removed when pruning. The shoots are cut 2–3 in (5–7 cm), leaving two or three leaves, and the lower half of the stem is inserted into the rooting medium. Roots will appear in three to four weeks.

3. Thick-stemmed

This is a relatively small group of 70 or so different species and hybrids not widely known or popular, being grown by collectors mainly for their curiosity value. As their name would suggest, they have thick stems from base to tip. They do make good container plants, but are fussy about good light. Some varieties can grow to 6 ft (1.8 m) in height even in containers. Therefore, care is needed when selecting which ones to grow. Almost all have large- to medium-sized leaves.

When propagating, the best results are obtained from leaf cuttings because of the thickness of the stems and the position of the leaves at the extremities of these. (Refer to Rex types for details of propagating techniques.)

Left: *Begonia parilis*, "Zigzag begonia", a thick-stemmed species that produces white flowers when given good light.

4. Trailing-scandents

Although there is not a wide selection in this group, they are well worth growing, particularly the fragrant types. Most of them originate from South America. The stems are long, and the leaves small. Some of the newer hybrids have attractively marked and colored leaves. They bloom in various seasons, and most have clusters of flowers. The Trailing-scandents often make good hanging basket plants, while others can be trained as climbers in and around the garden, depending on climatic conditions. They also make good houseplants. These begonias propagate very easily from tip and stem cuttings taken during pruning. Treat the cuttings as for Shrub-like.

5. Rhizomatous

Many hundreds of species and hybrids make this by far the largest group. Rhizomatous begonias are grown mainly for their attractive leaves and foliage. Mexico is the source of most, and quite a number of the early discoveries (before 1850) are still popular today, together with the many hybrids that have been developed.

Leaf colors, textures, patterns and size are highly varied, which is why they are so popular as houseplants. However, some varieties grow quite large, with leaves exceeding 18 in (45 cm), so are suitable only for the outdoors. Most of the flowers are insignificant and grow on long stems above the plant foliage. However, these can add to the beauty of the whole plant, especially as most flower in late winter and early spring when other plants are less obliging.

The characteristic rhizome of the species is a procumbent or subterranean, root-like stem, which produces roots from its lower surface and leaves and shoots from the upper. The group is subdivided into those with erect and those with creeping rhizomes,

Above: *Begonia solananthera*, a trailing-scandent, is suited to hanging baskets. Its fragrant flowers appear in winter-spring.

Right: *Begonia goegoensis*, the "Fire-king begonia", is rhizomatous, low-growing and has large leaves with red beneath.

Above: These flowers are typical of the cleft-leafed sub-group of Rhizomatous begonias.

the latter type tending to look both bushy and compact.

Overwatering these plants, especially during the winter months, tends to produce rot in the rhizome. The group prefers humidity at the higher end of the recommended scale for begonias (60–70 percent). A small amount of fertilizer can be given during active growth. Repotting is advisable only in the springtime.

Methods of propagation are the same as for the Rex Cultorum group (see page 20).

6. Rex Cultorum

In the 19th century, *B. rex* plants, grown solely for their foliage, were very highly sought after and were hybridized in the hundreds. Today's hybrids contain the genes of as many as 15 other species of begonias and the group, now consisting solely of hybrids, is known as Rex Cultorum. In the main, Rex Cultorum are rhizomatous, although some that were developed by crosses with tuberous and semi-tuberous begonias are not strictly so.

Because today's hybrids come from such a broad breeding spectrum, they are highly varied. These plants are grown solely for their foliage, which is truly magnificent. The colors of the leaves can range through green, red, pink and lavender to silver and even black. Although leaf size and growth habit is so diverse, they can be easily identified as a Rex by their distinctive leaf shape.

Rex begonias enjoy slightly warmer conditions, around 75°F (24°C); they do not like hot temperatures, but will survive down to 50°F (10°C) or lower, as long as they are not frosted. Their main love is humidity—generally around 60 percent is ideal, but some varieties like it even higher. This can be increased as previously described (see page 15). They also prefer high light levels but not direct sunlight. Good ventilation is essential to prevent attacks of mildew, and care when watering, to avoid wetting the leaves, will also help.

These plants do have a dormant period over the cooler winter months, when they prefer to be kept on the dry side and not given any supplementary food, but even at this time the humidity must be maintained. In the spring, plants should be repotted into a free-draining open mix; some coarse grit or

Left: *Begonia* 'Lorraine Closson', a striking dwarf Rex variety.

Pruning in the winter will keep the plants tidy. If the rhizome becomes dry and gnarled, it is best to replace the plant with one that is younger and more vigorous.

Plants can be propagated very easily by leaf cuttings or by stem cuttings from sections of the rhizome. Most growers prefer the leaf cutting, which, although somewhat slower, produces new plants in larger numbers.

Various methods can be used for taking the leaf cuttings:

a. Cut a leaf, shorten the stem, and insert it into a small container of sand, pumice or other propagating mix.

b. Nick the veins on the underside of a leaf, lay it on damp sand, and weight it down with pebbles to ensure the cuts contact the sand.

c. Cut a leaf in "V" sections from the stem to the outer edge and insert these wedges into the propagating mix.

In all cases, rooting should take three to four weeks. (Refer to Chapter 11 for other details on propagation.)

charcoal added to the mix will be helpful. Do not compress the mix with the fingers when repotting, but leave it light and fluffy.

In spring, biweekly feeds of a 20-20-20 NPK fertilizer at half strength may be given, but high-nitrogen fertilizers should be avoided so the plant stays tight and compact. As the summer progresses, the feeding should be reduced.

Leaf cuttings using V sections of a Rex variety, 'Fire Flush'.

After three weeks, roots are developing.

7. Semperflorens (Wax or Bedding begonias)

This group is the most widely known of all begonia types. As well as being popular with the home gardener, they make a wonderful mass display in public gardens and parks. The term Semperflorens aptly means "ever-flowering". Following the original crosses in 1878, hybridizing continued over many years to produce the Semperflorens varieties of today. The name Semperflorens Cultorum was adopted in 1945 for this group.

There are still a number of Semperflorens species obtainable, but, although some are dwarfish, most tend to be taller than the modern hybrids, growing up to 2 ft (60 cm) in some cases. These are grown mainly by people who specialize in original plants.

Semperflorens now come in a range of colors—catalog examples include white, clear pink, rose, white with margin (rose, scarlet, and salmon-red), salmon or salmon-orange. All have attractive foliage, with green, variegated or bronze available.

A spiral-planted formal display of Semperflorens in a public garden.

A recent introduction has been a double-flowered variety in pink, red or white. The Semperflorens hybrids generally grow to about 8 in (20 cm), allowing them to be effective as border plants.

As well as being grown en masse, Semperflorens make excellent container plants, either as a border around a large container or even inserted into spaghnum moss around the sides of hanging baskets, where they make an attractive display. They are equally as good in individual containers. So versatile are they, their use is only restricted by the whim of the grower.

Semperflorens must be grown in good light or they will become leggy and will not have the profusion of flowers we associate with them. They are relatively tolerant of heat, so can be grown in full sun, although it is preferable to accustom them gradually to these conditions.

Pink Semperflorens in a group of containers liven up a courtyard.

If planted in groups, a spacing of 8 in (20 cm) is required to allow the plants to spread. Semperflorens are bushy by nature, but pinching out the growing tips of the stems and the buds as they appear will significantly improve the quality of the blooms on each plant and will ensure that it will be very bushy and floriferous. This may be done up to three times, two weeks apart.

Semperflorens are fibrous-rooted, so in the main are treated as annual plants. However, in warmer climates, where there are no frosts, they can be cut back by about two-thirds if they become too tall or leggy, and they will grow again in a very short time. Even in areas where frosts may occur, such as zone 8, if grown in the garden, they can be covered with straw, which will give them protection, allowing them to regenerate again in the spring. If they have been grown in containers, they should be moved into shelter for the winter when frosts are anticipated, that is, when the temperature is forecast to drop to 24°F (5°C) and the weather is clear. If a heated greenhouse is available, the plants can be moved there for the winter months, thus ensuring continuous color.

Semperflorens grown in containers in a good potting mix to which sufficient controlled- release fertilizer has been added should require no further fertilizing; likewise in the garden bed, provided it has been well prepared and fertilized. If supplements are considered necessary, a weak dose of fertilizer with a high potassium content may be applied every three weeks.

As a group, they are susceptible to fungal diseases such as mildew and botrytis. A spraying program may be adopted to overcome this problem, particularly where there is a big variation between the day- and night-time temperatures. To further reduce the incidence of these diseases, refrain from overhead watering, which wets the foliage. A trickle or ground-soaking water system is recommended, as this keeps the root structure damp and cool and reduces the danger of fungal problems.

Propagation of the modern hybrid types is done mainly from seed, since they are so easy to grow. Cuttings may also be taken, or, when the plant is of a sufficient size, it may be divided using a sharp spade or knife. With the natural species, plant propagation is from cuttings, either by removing the tips or by taking basal shoots from around the base, with the best results achieved from basal cuttings (see Chapter 11).

Availability of Non-tuberous begonias

Cane-like, Rhizomatous, and Rex Cultorum: some hybrids are available in most nurseries as well as other outlets, such as supermarkets. Specialist nurseries also have a wide range of the better and newer hybrids.

Shrub-like and Trailing-scandents: specialist growers and nurseries.

Thick-stemmed: not generally available; grown mostly by collectors and hybridizers.

Semperflorens: Semperflorens plants and seeds are widely available at plant nurseries as well as many other outlets. Species are available from specialist sources.

For the frustrated collector, it is worth noting that species seed and seed from hybridization may be sourced from seed banks run by interest groups and clubs.

CHAPTER 3

Tuberous Begonias

The various forms of winter-flowering tuberous begonias in a colorful display.

With the exception of Semperflorens (Bedding begonias), tuberous begonias (*Begonia* Tuber-hybrida) are probably the type of begonia best-known and most widely-grown and enjoyed by the average gardener around the world. This was not always the case. For many years it was thought they were delicate plants that had to be grown in hot-houses. In fact, they may be grown successfully in suitable sites in the open garden, which puts them within the reach of most gardeners.

The tuberous root system of this group enables them to become dormant over the winter period and thus survive (when lifted and stored) and grow again when the weather becomes warmer. This winter dormancy permits a greater range of climate zones in which they may be grown outside, compared with the non-tuberous varieties (up to zones 2 and 3 in Canada, see page 33, Cold Zones).

Flower types

The development of the tuberous hybrids has brought us considerable variety of form, shape, and color. The following terms describe the flower types found within the group.

Picotee: The petals have a fine edge that is a different color from the main part of the flower. In describing a picotee, the ground or main color is

Above left: 'Jean Blair' is an example of a yellow-red picotee. Above right: This begonia has a perfect rose-form center. Left: An Antonelli bicolor.

Rose-form: This is a begonia with a flower center resembling a rosebud.

Ruffled: This describes flower petals that are wavy. They vary from the two forms above, which have flat petals.

Serrated: The petals on these flowers have serrated edges. This type is sometimes marketed as Lace begonias.

Sub-groups of tuberous begonias
Tuberous species

A number of tuberous species are still grown, though they are in general not widely available. Several of these—*Begonia boliviensis*, *B. cinnabarina*, *B. pearcei*, and *B. veitchii*—are described in Chapter 1 on the ancestors of tuberous begonias.

B. sutherlandii, which originates in South Africa, is pendulous in form. It has tiny, attractive, pale orange flowers, red stems and pale green foliage. It can grow to a large size—specimens more than 3 ft (1 m) across have been reported. Unfortunately, it has a tendency to mildew.

given first and the edge next, so 'Jean Blair' is a yellow-red picotee, or a picotee with a yellow main color and a fine red edge.

Bicolor: This describes a flower with two colors that merge, but where the edge is not defined enough to be classed as a picotee.

Camellia form: This refers to the shape of the flower, in which the center appears like a camellia flower. It is not seen in modern hybrids.

From China comes *Begonia grandis* ssp. *evansiana*, or the Hardy begonia. It has white flowers, tinted pink, and the heart-shaped leaves have red highlights.

The unusual *Begonia gracilis*, from Mexico, has been described as the Hollyhock begonia. It grows up to 3 ft (1 m) tall on an erect stem, with pink flowers on the stem and roundish leaves.

The above three plants produce bulbils in the leaf stem axils, which will reproduce if planted.

Finally comes *Begonia micranthera*, which was found in both Argentina and Bolivia. This tall-growing plant has orange-red flowers, and one variant is fragrant.

Above: *Begonia gracilis* var *martiana*, the "Hollyhock begonia".
Left: A group of *Begonia sutherlandii*.

Tuberous hybrids
Large-flowered Standards
These are the queens of the tuberous begonias, with their glowing colors, variety of form and long flowering season. They are standards (growing in an upright manner), and the most choice, the named hybrids, are generally grown in containers where the flowers may achieve sizes up to 8–9 in (20–22 cm).

Pendula, basket or cascade
The growth habit of these tuberous begonias is hanging or cascading, so they are usually grown in a basket. Flowers tend to be smaller than the standards, but the plants are very floriferous and make a splendid colorful sight when grown well.

Above left: Yellow Crispa-marginata.
Above right: A marbled Marmorata, a variety of which is known as 'Stars and Stripes' in the USA.

Fimbriata

These begonias have double flowers 5 in (12 cm) in diameter. The edge of each petal is frilled or fimbriated. They are often made more attractive by contrasting yellow stamens. Sometimes these are referred to as Ballerina or Carnation begonias. The first Fimbriata type was offered for sale in 1898, and, although not as popular today, they are still grown. They come in a full range of colors—red, copper, orange, pink, white and yellow.

Marginata

These have large 5–7 in (12–17 cm) flowers. The base color is white, and usually the perianth (or petal) shows a narrow pink to red margin. They are picotee versions of the early single begonias.

Crispa-marginata

Also known as the Fascination begonias, only two varieties are left in this group today: the yellow and the white. Both are single picotees and have a very fimbriated (or frilled) red edge and a marked cluster of yellow stamens in the center of each bloom. Though not widely grown, they add something different to any collection.

Marmorata

This variety has blotched or marbled petals with a white background on which are red, pink or occasionally orange splashes of color. They are almost identical in habit to the large, tuberous doubles but have flowers of only 4 in (10 cm).

Left: A white Fimbriata type.

Non-stop

Non-stops are an ideal plant for bedding purposes. Their maximum height is 8–10 in (20–25 cm), and they require no stakes. Flowers are from 2½–3 in (6–9 cm) in diameter and cover a full range of colors, including picotees.

Multiflora

The plants that fall into this category are tuberous varieties of a compact habit and, as their name suggests, with a multitude of blooms. In general, these flowers are single or semi-double and 1–1½ in (2.5–4 cm) in size. They stand well above the foliage. These hybrids are ideal in borders, in containers or tubs, or even in hanging baskets. They are somewhat hardier than their larger cousins, for they will stand more sun and heat, and they seem more resistant to diseases such as powdery mildew.

Of the large number of Multifloras that were bred in continental Europe, sadly, only a small proportion still remains. Those still in cultivation are 'Helen Harmes', a semi-double bright yellow; 'Le Flamboyant' (often referred to as simply 'Flamboyant'), a single scarlet; 'Madame Richard Galle', a semi-double apricot; 'Le Madelon', with single pink flowers; and finally, one that has recently re-emerged, 'Gents Juweeltje' ('Jewel of Ghent'), with semi-double, apricot-orange flowers.

A Multiflora variety, marketed as 'Burgermaster', is also occasionally available. These are slightly taller and have a profusion of small, semi-double flowers in pink, red, lemon, apricot or yellow.

Another sub-group, the Multiflora Maxima, is very similar in habit to the Multifloras but has larger flowers of up to 3 in (7.5 cm) in size.

A range of fully double Minis, similar to the Multifloras, have also been developed by Antonelli's of California in a wide range of colors, including some picotees.

Bertinii Compacta

'Christrose' and 'Sonnenschein' were both introduced into Germany in 1962 by Joseph Rothmund and are classified as part of the Bertinii Compacta Group. Both are singles; 'Christrose' is white with a red-veined center and 'Sonnenschein' is yellow with a red-veined center. They are very floriferous

Below left: 'Helen Harmes', a Multiflora in a hanging basket.
Below right: 'Sonnenschein', a Bertinii Compacta.

A winter-flowering begonia.

with flowers about 1 in (2.5 cm) across, which hold themselves up above the foliage.

Winter-flowering

The introduction and development of the winter-flowering begonias, such as Hiemalis and Cheimantha, was carried out mainly in Europe. These plants introduced the possibility of having begonias flowering indoors year-round. They have been developed specifically as houseplants, tolerating conditions that most other tuberous begonias dislike and give that much-needed touch of color in the winter months.

They do not hibernate in the winter as do true tuberous begonias (perhaps because one of their ancestors is a bulbous winter-flowering type), and their care differs a little from that of the other tuberous types, so is described here. In fact, while accepting Thompson's eight categories, it may be said that this sub-group fits least well into its designated section and almost merits a grouping of its own. Even their "tubers" appear to be almost as much a rhizome as a tuber in appearance.

They are very susceptible to overwatering, so they should be grown in open, free-draining potting mix and kept as dry as possible. If well-fed and grown in reasonable light, they will smother themselves in 1 in (2.5 cm) semi-double flowers, ranging from scarlet through to soft pastels, pinks and creams. A lot of growers in Europe treat these plants as annuals, but with care, one can obtain many seasons of growth from them. At the end of the winter-flowering period, the plants can be cut back by about one-third and placed somewhere cool, but with reasonable light, to await fall when they will put on growth and flower once again. During this period the plants must be kept very dry. When the plants show signs of new growth in the fall, they may be repotted.

The only means of increasing stock is by vegetative cuttings, since these plants are sterile. The technique is the same as for tuberous begonias (see Chapter 11).

Fragrant varieties

Although there are a number of fragrant species of begonia, very few of these are tuberous. Modern hybrids, too, mostly lack scent. However, as a result of a deliberate breeding program, some scented tuberous hybrids are now gradually being developed and are becoming available. They generally have a delicate citrus perfume, which becomes more apparent in warm conditions.

In the late 1930s, an American grower, Leslie Woodriff, crossed two tuberous species, *Begonia baumannii* and *B. micranthera fimbriata*, and produced a scented hybrid that he called 'Wild Rose'. He then crossed 'Wild Rose' with an unnamed, large-flowered Pendula and produced a number of scented seedlings, of which only 'Yellow Sweety' (sometimes misnamed as 'Sweetie') remains in cultivation today.

In 1981, Howard Siebold, also from the United States, started hybridizing some of his own plants with 'Yellow Sweety'. Siebold was successful in pro-

'Yellow Sweety', an early fragrant variety, bred in North America.

ducing a number of new, scented Pendula hybrids, one of which, 'Sweet Dianne', won an American Begonia Society Gold Medal. Another of Howard Siebold's fragrant basket varieties, 'Pink Spice', is commercially available today. However, very few upright varieties carry fragrance to any degree.

Siebold then began distributing seed from his crosses to interested growers around the world to give a larger growing base. Several New Zealand growers have been involved in the program. Ian McNeur of Wanganui has had particular success and has produced a number of fragrant hybrids, both Pendula and Large-flowered upright, which he has named. He has also been working with some success in developing fragrance in what he classes as "minis", small-growing varieties for planters and the garden.

Siebold also sent seed to Blackmore & Langdon in the United Kingdom and I understand they will shortly be releasing their first fragrant variety. This work is in the early development phase and something for growers to look forward to. Availability of Blackmore & Langdon fragrant varieties in North America will depend on specialist nurseries or growers importing and propagating them, which may, in turn, depend on public demand.

Availability of tuberous begonias

The species are mostly available only from specialist sources or other collectors. However, *Begonia sutherlandii* is advertised in some plant catalogs.

Winter-flowering begonias are readily available from many outlets, including even supermarkets, as are Multiflora Maxima. Seed for the latter is also available at some selected seed merchants. With Non-stops, both seed and small plants ready to plant out in spring are freely available.

Fimbriatas can be grown from either seed or tubers. Seed can be purchased in each of the individual colors.

Marmorata seed can be obtained from selected seed merchants, and in the spring, seedlings are available at some begonia nurseries.

Unnamed varieties of both standard and Pendula begonias are available from many nurseries. See Appendix 2 for details on specialist sources, e.g., for named varieties of Standards or Pendulas, and the more unusual types such as Marginata, Crispa-marginata, Multifloras, Bertinii Compacta and other species.

CHAPTER 4

Cultivation of Tuberous Begonias

General requirements

As mentioned in earlier chapters, the tuberous root system of these begonias enables them to become dormant over winter. This means tubers can be lifted and stored. When the growing season approaches, they can then be potted either in containers for outdoor display, or placed in the garden once the weather is warm enough for flowering to begin. So, the environments in which tuberous begonias are grown include the garden, the greenhouse and shadehouse, and conservatory. Wherever they are, matters such as air circulation, humidity, water and light need to be considered. Arguably the most important of these is air circulation.

Air circulation

Tuberous begonias prefer cool to moderate temperatures and will struggle at anything constantly above 86°F (30°C), whether indoors or out. Furthermore, the one thing they thrive on above all else is good air circulation; therefore, plants must not be overcrowded. Good spacing is critical to prevent stagnant air, for this predisposes the plants to fungal diseases such as botrytis and powdery mildew, especially toward the latter part of the season when night temperatures drop and humidity is still high.

While they enjoy good airflow, Tuberhybrida may be damaged by excessive wind and marked by heavy rain. The best results, particularly worth the effort with the better quality plants such as named begonias, will be achieved with some form of pro-

tection. If you are growing indoors during the flowering season, obviously protection from the elements won't be a concern.

But if your collection is very large and you want perfect blooms, you will need some form of specific shelter designed to house plants. The choice of this shelter depends largely on the climate. A greenhouse will give full protection from the elements and, if heated, will protect also from unseasonable cold, although this adds to the cost. Thus, in some colder areas, a greenhouse may still be the preferred location to grow tuberous begonias. An added advantage for people who grow for show competition and want perfect blooms is the protection it affords from flying insects. A shadehouse is also an option if you want to protect your plants during the growing season.

Returning, then, to the issue of providing good airflow, the use of a greenhouse presents several problems. On hot days, some means of forced ventilation is desirable, as well as shading (such as blinds) to prevent burning. Ideally the ventilation should be automated; otherwise, someone should be available to watch for sudden temperature fluctuations. Unfortunately, the smaller the space the harder it is to control the environment.

A shadehouse has the advantage of providing excellent ventilation, while judicious placement of the shadecloth filters the wind and provides protection from direct sunlight. If the shadehouse is built with some form of permanent roofing material such as corrugated plastic, there will be maximum protection against rain, yet at the same time a good amount of light. (Plastic containing flecks of rein-

Opposite: White lobelias and variegated vinca vine contrast well with begonias.

forcing material is best avoided, for this cuts down on the available light.)

In terms of cost, a shadehouse is cheaper to build and run than a greenhouse. Generally the structure is built of wood, with shadecloth walls stapled to the framing. Shadecloth comes in various colors and densities; 30–50 percent cloth is ideal for begonias, but no heavier. The knitted type of cloth, though it is somewhat more expensive than the woven, is much stronger and does not fray when cut.

Humidity

Begonias love a humid atmosphere whether indoors or out, but it must be associated with warmth. Warm and damp are fine, but cold and damp spell disaster. During spring and fall, humidity is easily achieved—the difficulty for plants outdoors is often the lack of warmth because of the cooler evening and night-time temperatures. In summer the opposite applies—plenty of heat, but a lack of moisture. During the hottest part of the day, watering the soil around the plants (not the plants themselves) will help. Indoors, placing the containers on or next to a tray of pebbles half-filled with water will also put more moisture into the air (check the water level

A custom-made shadehouse using shadecloth walls and plastic roofing.

regularly). Maintaining reasonable humidity is often the most difficult aspect of growing begonias in a conservatory, as most other occupants prefer a drier environment. If a shadehouse or greenhouse is used, watering the floor will rectify any humidity problems. Do not extend this past mid-afternoon, to allow for a reduction in air moisture with the onset of cooler evenings.

Light

Like all begonias, Tuberhybrida require good light, but whatever their situation, they do need some shade. They will tolerate direct early morning or late afternoon sun, but will burn badly if exposed to the extreme heat around midday. Be careful where you place your plants. A situation too near a south-facing window in summer can cause extreme temperatures. Good light levels will ensure that the plants flower well, thus producing the vibrant, colorful blooms they are renowned for. Poor light will inhibit flowering, resulting in small blooms with poor color and the plants will become tall and spindly.

Water

A frequent question is, "How often should I water my begonias?" and it is a difficult one to answer. Factors to consider are type of growing medium, the environment in which the plants are grown (including humidity), size of the plant and container, and, if outdoors, weather conditions.

For example, a large plant with many flowers and a container full of roots can easily cope with a good watering every day in warm weather, and maybe even twice a day on very hot days. On the other hand, a freshly potted plant with a small root system in a proportionately larger container will take a few days before regular watering is required.

One thing is certain—more begonias of all types are killed by overwatering than through any other cause, so if in doubt, DON'T. A good general rule is that if the mix is already wet, then further moisture is not required. (For more details on watering, including automatic systems, see Chapter 10.)

Other factors that are important for successful growing of Tuberhybrida are the choice of potting mix and feeding (see Chapter 9) and the prevention and control of disease (Chapter 8).

Growing in difficult conditions

The key thing to remember is that the basic requirements of the plants remain the same; in anything less than the ideal situation, the grower should be seeking to modify local conditions to suit.

Cold zones

All begonias, as previously mentioned, are susceptible to frost. However, they can still be grown in the harsher areas of the globe, such as climatic zones 2 and 3 in Canada, albeit for a shorter season, if given protection.

If the dormant tubers of tuberous begonias are lifted before the ground freezes and brought on indoors to start flowering, they can be planted outside for the short and intense flowering season, if the necessary 60°F (15°C) is maintained during this

This greenhouse is used for growing begonias year-round in a cold zone.

time. Experiments have shown that by giving a plant sufficient light and some warmth, they will continue to grow and flower.

Of all begonias, tuberous begonias are the best suited to colder zones because of their winter dormancy. In such areas, the warm summer months are greatly reduced. The plants, whether for container culture or the garden, need to be grown in a protected environment, especially at night, for an extended period until conditions are frost-free.

The use of a heated greenhouse, plastic tunnel house, or other protective structure that can be heated, during the colder months, is a great advantage, but use can also be made of rooms within one's home. In this case, additional lighting may be needed, especially if the plants are growing in a heated basement.

If grown close to a south-facing window, they would have adequate light, but protection from burning with the use of sheer curtains may be necessary. In all these situations, additional ventilation with fans should be considered.

As soon as conditions are warm enough, the plants should be gradually hardened off for several weeks by placing them outside during the day and

Raised beds are used to display begonias effectively in this courtyard garden.

returning them to cover at night. After this, varieties intended for garden beds can be planted out and the containers safely left outside. Although the summer season is very short, the greater length of the daylight hours helps to counteract this by intensifying both the color and the quality of the blooms.

Hot zones

Such areas, being frost-free, may provide suitable conditions, at least in terms of temperature, for the non-tuberous begonias.

But tuberous varieties are not very tolerant of extreme heat and generally do not grow well if the daytime temperature constantly exceeds 86°F (30°C). That is not to say they cannot be grown successfully in hot conditions, even in areas where the daytime temperature may reach as high as 105°F (40°C).

In these locations, extra shading needs to be provided and, of course, excellent ventilation.

Some growers also use humidifiers, and one I know channels cool air from her air conditioning unit into her begonia area. Extra care is also required with watering to prevent the plants from drying out too quickly.

Displaying your plants

No matter how many plants you have, in the garden or in containers, consideration must be given not only to their culture but also to their display, to get the maximum benefit from their beauty.

In the garden, after selecting a suitable semi-shaded position, the use of a raised bed will elevate the plants and, as a bonus, eliminate the need for bending. Another idea is to use a natural slope, preferably terraced. Such an area is ideal, for it lifts the blooms closer to eye level, giving a better view of them. Either way, if more than one row of plants is being displayed, the back row should be mounded up or taller varieties placed at the rear.

I have adopted both of these principles in my front garden. The garden faces east and is shaded by a large variegated elm tree. It has a natural slope of about 3 ft (1 m) down to sidewalk level. The top has been terraced to give two separate levels, in front of which it slopes down to a low stone wall.

Containers planted with begonias and strategically placed are ideal to give points of emphasis and continuity between the display and surrounding areas. Where possible, planting blocks of similar colors is effective.

Both in the garden and in containers, there are a number of companion plants that are a perfect counterfoil to begonias. The delicate leaves and flowers of

may simply be placed on a table on the patio or in the conservatory.

Shelving is a simple and not-too-expensive way to display containers in a small area. I have free-standing, two-tier shelving running the whole length of the outside of my house. As the shelves are against the house, the plants are given good protection from sun and rain by the eaves. Each shelf is 10 in (25 cm) wide and staggered, with each level 10 in (25 cm) higher than the one below, although the size can be adjusted to suit the size of the container.

Larger collections generally require a custom-built shadehouse or, in colder climates where the growing season is short, a greenhouse with appropriate shelving. These can be as big as the builder's imagination or finance or space allows. However, it is not necessary to have a huge shadehouse to display your plants to their best advantage.

Recognizing quality in Tuberhybrida

When I first started to grow tuberous begonias, I had no appreciation of what was a good plant or flower. If it grew well and was colorful, it was okay

lobelias are ideal, and the trailing varieties are good in container arrangements. The range of colors allows for some pleasing combinations. Ferns are another good contrast, and I use maidenhair ferns in containers between my named varieties, as their delicate fronds contrast well with the solid leaves of the begonias. An added advantage is that my begonia containers are spaced at a good distance.

Deciding how to display begonias in containers will depend on the number and the space available. As with garden varieties, it is better if the blooms are elevated closer to eye level—a few containers by me. I have learned a lot since that time from reading and talking to many people and from observations of the flowers I grow.

Named begonias quickly supplanted my initial collection of garden-center begonias as I came to appreciate the improved performance and higher quality of these beauties. In my early enthusiasm, I bought every named one I could get my hands on, but soon, two things happened. First, I ran out of space (especially when I started hybridizing and needed room for seedlings). Second, my palate became more refined, and I became selective in my approach, rather than eclectic.

So, what makes a good plant or flower, and what other aspects should be considered in putting together a personal collection?

The plant

Begonias are no different from any other plant in that their growth needs to be vigorous. Vigor, however, does not mean that a plant should grow to enormous size, but rather that it produces strong, healthy growth.

A strong resistance to disease is also important. Some plants are particularly susceptible to powdery mildew, no matter what steps are taken to combat it. Such plants should never be used for hybridization and need to be monitored carefully if kept in the collection.

The flower

It is said that beauty is in the eye of the beholder, and this is certainly true with begonias. Some people admire single flowers or those with no formal center, which are full of pollen. I would not give such flowers shelf room. To me, a good flower, and one to be sought, is that described by Brian Langdon in his book *Begonias, The Care and Cultivation of Tuberous Varieties*. He suggests there are four things to look for in a high-quality begonia flower. These are: good depth of flower from front to back (see opposite); good breadth of the individual petals; "heavy" petal texture with a silk-like effect; and the shape or form of the flower, which should be full—but not crowded—and without a muddled center. Although good size is also important, in general it takes second place to quality. Beyond this, the flower needs to have good keeping qualities so that a large number of flowers will be fully open on the plant at one time.

Langdon is, of course, discussing standard Tuberhybrida here. With Pendulas, the comments still apply, but on a smaller scale. Of equal importance is that the plant should be very floriferous, and that the stems hang well and do not break off easily.

Other considerations

Local conditions—for example, climate or growing area—are factors that also need to be taken into account. Experience will show that some plants are more robust and will cope better than others with heat, damp, and other trying conditions.

Personal preference is a final and important consideration. There is no point in growing a color or shape you don't like. However, with such a wide range of shapes, colors, and growth habits, there is always something for everybody.

Concerning named varieties

Named varieties have in the past been hard to get and generally expensive. Thus, many people have preferred to grow garden varieties only and have achieved satisfying and wonderful massed displays from these. Nevertheless, named begonias are considered to be superior to the run-of-the-mill plants, and there are good reasons for this.

Named begonias are the result of stringent selection from seedlings in a specific program that have been grown and flowered in a controlled environment. A small number of these with potential may be selected, to be grown again the following season. An example of this process comes from the Blackmore & Langdon Nursery in England. They grow around 100,000 plants from seed each year and may

select only five or six for continuation in the program. Eventually, after adequate trialing for consistency and quality, the chosen few are given a name and henceforth propagation is by vegetative means to ensure continuity, since they do not come true from self-pollination.

In North America, some Blackmore & Langdon named varieties are available from specialist sources as well as the North American-developed "San" and "Santa" series (see Appendix 2).

It is just as easy to grow a good plant as a bad one —this is equally true of all plants—so maybe you should consider starting a collection of named varieties, no matter how small.

A note on importing

Tubers and plant material can be sent around the world, provided specific strict measures are applied. These measures vary depending on the country

Note the good depth from front to back of this lovely flower.

involved. It is therefore very important to inquire with either the local agricultural authority or Customs office to ensure compliance with each country's regulations. Failure to do so could result in prosecution or confiscation of tubers or plants, or both (see Appendix 2).

When tubers are imported by growers and cross the hemisphere boundary, the growing system needs to take into account the seasonal disruption.

Coming from the southern hemisphere winter to a northern summer, tubers are generally started straight away. They usually oblige quite well, but as the season draws to a close, these imported plants are just coming into their prime. It is therefore desirable to grow them on right through the winter. To do so requires light and warmth, with the light

'Fairylight'

'Primrose'

'Roy Hartley'

'Pink Champagne'

'Tahiti'

'Zulu'

span being at least 14, preferably 16 hours in each 24, especially if the plants are to flower. The following spring, new growth shoots emerge from the base of the main stem. The plant is grown on for a further season and the old foliage removed. This system may be successfully applied to any importation of tubers from one hemisphere to the other.

Some suggestions for your collection

More than 1000 varieties have been named over the years, and available varieties do change from year-to-year. The following suggestions are the most up-to-date at the time of publication and would give a good foundation to any collection.

Large-flowered standards

'Allan Langdon'. Cardinal-red. Lovely rose-form blooms.

'Amy'. Rose-pink. Rose-form flowers.

'Billie Langdon'. A good clear white with flowers that stand out against the dark green foliage.

'Fairylight'. Cream-red picotee. Delicate to look at, and the flowers are long-lasting.

'Gypsy Maiden'. A most unusual salmon-pink.

'Jean Blair'. A yellow-red picotee.

'Lancelot'. A good clear white.

'Mardi Gras'. A strong-growing picotee, in white with a distinct red edge.

'Memories'. Soft coral-pink blooms on a tall-growing plant.

'Nell Gwynne'. Unusual creamy peach coloring.

'Pink Champagne'. White with the faintest touch of pink.

'Primrose'. As its name suggests, primrose-yellow in color. A shorter-growing plant.

'Roy Hartley'. Large flowers of salmon-pink that always make a fine display.

'Sea Coral'. Coral-pink. A stocky grower.

'Sugar Candy'. Pink, and an old favorite.

'Tahiti'. Coral-apricot. A reliable variety with vibrant colors that is good for beginners.

'Zulu'. Very deep crimson with rose-shaped flowers.

'Champagne'

'Lou Anne'

Pendulas

'Apricot Cascade'. Apricot shades. A favorite that produces many flowers.

'Champagne'. A free-flowering basket from Belgium.

'Lou Anne'. A pretty pink basket. An older introduction, but still popular.

'Ophelia'. A basket with white-apricot blooms. A strong grower that makes a fine display.

'Pink Spice'. A fragrant variety developed by Howard Siebold.

'Yellow Sweety'. One of the early fragrant varieties developed by Leslie Woodriff, and still popular.

CHAPTER 5

Large-flowered Tuberhybrida in Containers through the Year

The start of the growing year for a tuberous begonia is spring, when the tubers are still dormant. The tubers will be of various sizes and the largest is not necessarily the best, as very large plants can come from very small tubers.

Budding up

Before starting the tubers, two steps must be taken. First, inspect them all thoroughly to make sure they are healthy. Next is the step called budding up, where the buds or "pinkies" are encouraged to appear by moving the tubers from the cool area where they have been stored into a warmer environment.

The decision on when and how to start tubers into growth for the new season depends on location, personal preference, and the type of facilities available. Although not essential, having good facilities such as an area of bottom heat will assist greatly in being able to get tubers off to an early start, thus extending the flowering season. Where the tubers are placed for budding up does not matter as long as it is warm, e.g., near but not on a furnace. Do this early only if bottom heat, such as a heating pad, is available for the next step.

Some growers use a further treatment to assist budding up. Before any buds are showing, the tubers are immersed in warm water maintained at 115°F (46°C) for 15 minutes. Immediately following this,

Opposite: A plant grown with three stems for an all-around display.

Buds or "pinkies" on tubers that have been stored. Note the securely fastened labels.

they are placed in cold water for a similar time. They are then placed, uncovered, in a warm environment, as above. This treatment is believed to encourage the buds by softening the outer layer of the tuber, and to be beneficial in killing any pests that are still present. It was specifically introduced for problems with the leaf eelworm in the U.K. and then was shown to hasten the appearance of buds. If using this method, it is most important that neither time nor temperature is exceeded.

Prior to the formation of buds, other treatments may be used to assist in plumping the tubers and also with pest and disease control. The first is the sterilization of tubers in a bleach solution of ten parts of cold water to one part of bleach. The tubers

The reward for taking a little care: a colorful display.

are soaked for up to 15 minutes and then rinsed in clean, fresh water. Bleach is widely used as a sterilizing agent in plant tissue culture, and this treatment is thought to kill off any harmful pathogens, insects or mites without damaging the tuber. The second method is to dip the tubers in cold water to which an insecticide/fungicide or miticide has been added according to manufacturer's instructions.

Sometimes, healthy tubers are reluctant to bud up. If any tubers fail to show signs of a bud after a month or so in the warm, yet are still firm and not obviously rotten, give them the fingernail test. This involves gently lifting a small piece of the tuber's skin with a fingernail. If the flesh looks brown, whether mushy or dry, rot is present. If, however, the flesh looks green, or sometimes pink, all is well. Return it to the warmth and above all have patience. Sometimes a tuber tossed aside because it would not get going has been found weeks later growing well.

When the buds are about $^1/_4$ in (0.50 cm) high, it is time to start the tuber. Do not forget to check them; otherwise, the shoots will grow long and weak, just like a potato found at the back of the cupboard!

Starting tubers

The most important requirement for the medium used to start tubers into growth is excellent drainage. Often, a plain mix of 50/50 peat and coarse sand is recommended on the grounds that the delicate early roots may be easily burned by a normal concentration of fertilizers. In this case, all the initial growth comes from the energy stored within the tuber, since in such a mix there are few nutrients for the plant to use.

In my experience, the use of good fresh potting mix with the addition of up to 40 percent coarse sand, pumice, perlite or vermiculite gives the benefit of both good drainage and nourishment to the plant right from the start.

Most custom-made mixes available today have slow-release fertilizer in them. Because the fertilizer is released in minute amounts, there is no danger of the young roots being damaged, the more so since the amount of fertilizer is relatively less, because of the added sand or pumice, etc.

Old potting mix should NOT be used, nor should the tubers be started in last season's mix if they have been left in their containers over the winter. These containers will almost certainly contain a high level of harmful salts that accumulated the previous season, and the new roots put out by the tuber will quickly burn off, leading to very poor, stunted growth. The reaction then, by the grower, may be to apply more water to the poorly performing plant, which would result in the tuber rotting, as the plant cannot use this moisture.

Place the mix in containers or trays at least 2½ in (6 cm) deep, and place them directly on a heat source if it is available. If a heat source is not available, place the containers in a warm, well-lit situation.

The budded-up tubers may now be pushed into the prepared mix, bud side up. They should have at least 2 in (5 cm) space all around to allow for good

Below left: Tubers placed in a tray to start, before covering over with extra mix.
Below right: Started tubers at various stages of growth; the larger ones are ready to be potted.

root growth and should then be thinly covered with additional mix to encourage them to grow roots over their whole surface.

The mix should now be checked for moisture by using a moisture meter or by pushing a finger down into it. If it is damp at the bottom, do not water; if dry, water lightly. It is most important to avoid overwatering, especially if bottom heat is lacking.

Potting

Traditionally, advice is given to move the growing plant into a larger container as it increases in size, but why not place the tuber in its final container right from the start and save all the work?

With large tubers this will be quite satisfactory and give good results. Large tubers develop, or should develop, a large root mass and more top growth. This means they can deal with a greater volume of mix and water. (Note that, if single potting is employed, tuber placement and staking should be as in Final Potting and Staking, see page 45.)

Smaller tubers, since they have a smaller root mass, will be swamped if planted directly into an 8 in

(20 cm) container. The small plants may not cope, particularly if the weather is cool and growth slow. Do not be tempted to use containers that are too large.

The first potting should be done when the top growth has reached 3–4 in (7–10 cm). The container should be large enough to hold the root ball with 1 in (2.5 cm) of space all around. Do not press the mix down too firmly, as the young roots are very tender. Gently knock the container on the bench to settle the mix, and then water.

Overwatering should be avoided at this stage while growth is slow. This is particularly so for those who live in cooler areas and those who use plastic containers, as in both cases, transpiration is less. When the plants are unable to transpire, the excess water in the mix causes the roots to rot, which leads to retarded growth and may ultimately cause the tuber to rot also.

Choice of containers for standard begonias

When choosing suitable containers, remember that good drainage is essential. In the past, placing pebbles or broken pieces of clay pots in the base of the container was necessary for good drainage, but with today's open, free-draining potting mixes this is no longer necessary. However, do make sure that the selected containers have enough holes in the bottom to allow a free flow of moisture, to keep the mix from compacting in the base of the container.

The size of container will depend on the age and size of the tuber, but in general I use a maximum of 8 in (20 cm) containers for my mature, named Tuberhybrida.

Containers can be either square or round, with the latter seeming to be more popular. Square containers hold a greater amount of potting mix relative to their surface area than do their round counterparts. Clay containers are very sturdy, but they are often more expensive than plastic. Their greater weight helps to keep plants from falling over, but they are more difficult to move around,

especially when they hold large plants. They are also more difficult to keep clean, and plants dry out more quickly, because the moisture in the mix evaporates both from the surface and through the clay walls. This can be overcome by painting the inside of each container with a water-based paint or with a silicone spray. There is something appealing about the appearance of a plant in a clean terracotta container.

Plastic containers, on the other hand, are less likely to break if dropped, though they will deteriorate and become brittle if left exposed to sunlight for long periods. Hygiene is easier with plastic containers, as they may be washed out in hot, soapy water, and they do not stain as readily as clay. A disadvantage is that they are lighter, causing problems if plants are allowed to dry out late in the season when the plant is top-heavy and may tip over.

Shaping the plant

In the early stage of growth, consider the number of shoots to be allowed to grow to maturity on each standard plant. In the case of multiple stems, some may, or should, be removed. Smaller first- and second-year tubers do better if only one stem is left to grow to maturity; multiple shoots will result in weak stems and smaller flowers. Also, a young tuber feeding many shoots is less able to increase its own size toward the end of the season.

On larger tubers, it is best to allow only two shoots, or possibly three, to grow on and flower. These need to be selected carefully for vigor and for the final look of the plant. The less vigorous should be removed, as should those facing the wrong direction.

Begonia stems have a back and front, with the flowers forming and facing forward within the arc of the leaf points, i.e., the pointed ends of the leaves indicate the front of the plant. It makes no sense, therefore, to retain a stem where the flowers are going to face inward toward the center of the plant. Where the plant is intended for all-around display, three to four evenly spaced shoots facing outward will give the best results.

The surplus shoots may simply be "rubbed off". However, they can provide a cheap and productive way to increase stock by using them as cutting material, and they are the easiest type of cutting to propagate. (See Chapter 11 on propagation techniques.)

Preventing disease

General hygiene is the best preventive measure. Clean your containers and other equipment at the start of the season and regularly clear fallen blooms and leaves during the season. This will help avoid such things as botrytis and mildew, as will good spacing of plants.

Because of the large number of named tubers in my stock, I use a specific program to minimize risk. When the plants are 3–4 in (7–10 cm) tall, I begin spraying with a miticide combined with a systemic fungicide/insecticide to cover other possible infections. I spray every two weeks until I decide not to remove any more buds and to let the plants flower. I do not spray again once flowering has started, unless there is a drastic need. (See Chapter 8 on pests and diseases.)

Feeding

I prefer to use a slow-release fertilizer in my potting mix, with the only supplement being a foliar feed early in the season to augment the nitrogen in the early growth period. (For details see Chapter 9.)

Final potting and staking

If plants are being potted in stages, their readiness for the next stage may be checked after four to six weeks by knocking them out of their containers. When the roots are beginning to show around the outside of the mix, then it is time to move up a container size. The plant should not be left until it is rootbound, as this will retard growth. The second

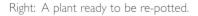
Right: A plant ready to be re-potted.

Above: Surplus shoots have been removed leaving just one main stem to grow; extra stakes support the side shoots.

Above: A plant repotted with the stake in place. The points of the leaves face the front and a clip secures the stake to the container.
Below: Stakes and soft ties support the plant as it grows.

potting may well be the last—if not, be prepared to take that extra step. The mechanics are exactly the same.

In this move, the container should allow at least another 1 in (2.5 cm) all around the root ball, or a little more for larger tubers. Smaller tubers of 1 in (2.5 cm) diameter can be flowered in 6 in (15 cm) containers, and larger ones in 8 in (20 cm), with the old grandaddy in 10 in (25 cm). Remember that the larger the container the heavier it is, and thus the more difficult to move around, especially if clay containers are used. With this final move, the top of the root ball should be set down about 2 in (5–6 cm) below the rim of the new container. This allows for later top-dressing as the fine surface roots appear and the mix compacts down with watering.

Where possible, the tuber should be set more toward the back of the container, if there is such a thing in a circle. Placing a stake now, just before putting the plant in the container will avoid damage to the tuber and roots. If staking is done at the time of final potting, whether this is the first potting or the last of a series, there will be no further disturbance to the plant, which should be tied right from this point. Setting the tuber toward the rear allows the support to be placed against the back and bottom of the container, thus giving greater stability.

As plants grow to full maturity with a good crop of large flowers, they become top-heavy, and even stems as thick as 1½ in (4 cm) or more will snap if the plant is moved unsupported. Square stakes about ½ in (1 cm) in size get a firmer grip in the mix and therefore give better support than round stakes. Place the stake against the back of the container but clear of the tuber and leaning slightly backward away from the plant. Small wire clips placed around the stake and slipped over the top lip of the container also help prevent the stake from moving.

When the plant is being grown with more than one stem, a stake will be required for each stem. Multiple stakes should be placed slightly outward

Right: The two smaller flowers (females with seed pods) on each side of the male flower bud are to be removed.

away from the center in a slight V. This helps open up the plant for better air movement, thus lessening disease and enhancing the display of the flowers.

As the stems grow, tie them loosely to the stakes at regular intervals, using a soft tying material, preferably green in color. Check regularly to make sure that the material does not cut into the stem as the plant grows.

Securing the buds

This term is often seen in books on tuberous begonias. In a non-show context, it simply means leaving the flower buds on once the plant has at least eight to ten leaves, having removed all of them until then. This ensures that both the plant and its root system are large enough to support and provide nutrients for the flowers. In the case of hanging baskets (see Chapter 6, Basket Begonias), the procedure is slightly different.

At this point it is possible to estimate when the first flowers will be fully open. Buds measuring just over 1 in (2.5 cm) at their widest point will take a further 30–40 days to open fully, depending somewhat on the variety and the weather.

Each larger center bud is flanked on either side by two smaller ones. The main center bud is always a double (male) flower and the two smaller ones usually single (female), although sometimes one is another smaller male. These two smaller buds should be removed as soon as possible to help increase the size of the center double flower. (Again, baskets and garden plants differ—see the following chapters.)

Top-dressing

Throughout this period of growth, as the mix compacts down, approximately 1 in (2.5 cm) of fresh mix may be spread in the container around the base of the plant. Such a top-dressing, done two or three

Right: The two smaller flowers (females with seed pods) on each side of the male flower bud are to be removed.

times during the season, will increase the nutrient supply available to the established plant.

The height of the season

As the plant continues to grow and the flowers increase in size, it is helpful to use some form of flower support for each bloom. The large size of some of the flowers is not always matched by strength of stem, and the impact of the display will be heightened by lifting the blooms and making sure they are facing forward at all times. Although commercially available at some outlets, supports can be made easily from plastic-coated wire. For ease of use, it is best if their length is adjustable. They require a large "U" at the top, which cradles the flower stalk immediately behind the bloom. As the plants grow, the support can be adjusted every day or so, taking care not to damage or break the blooms (see photograph on page 48).

General maintenance, such as deadheading and the removal of decaying foliage, is necessary throughout the season to maintain the impact of the display and prevent disease.

Above: Telescopic flower supports.
Opposite: 'Annette', well-displayed for a great show.

Whether the display is large or small, these are the months to enjoy the outstanding beauty of the Large-flowered Tuberhybrida.

Winding down for winter

As fall progresses, the plants, after several months of flowering, are approaching the end of the season, and the flowers greatly diminish in size. This period is very important in the growth cycle of a begonia, for now the plant turns the energy it once put into making beautiful flowers into increasing the size of the tuber and storing energy for start-up the following season.

To make sure that the tuber ripens properly and to assist with wintering over, each plant may be given a dose of sulfate of potash. Mix 1 tablespoon (15 g) into 1 gallon (4 L) of water and, using the solution, water each plant normally. If supplementary feeding has been used during the season, it should be stopped now.

Once the plant has ceased producing good blooms, it should be stopped by removing the plant's growing tip and those of any side shoots that have been allowed to grow and flower. At the same time, remove all remaining flowers and buds. The whole stem and foliage should not be cut off to encourage dormancy. In fact, the plants should be kept growing as long as possible, taking care to give only small amounts of water to help this last growth. Gradually as the weather turns colder and the days shorten, the plant will signal its intention to go dormant when its foliage and stems turn yellow and drop off. At this point, watering must be stopped. (In warmer climates, where natural dormancy is harder to achieve, it may be necessary as a last resort to cut the stem off approximately 6 in (15 cm) above soil level and cease watering.)

As the leaves and stems drop, the standard of hygiene must be maintained by clearing the fallen pieces so that rot does not start at the very bottom of the stem and infect the tuber.

As the foliage falls off, lay the containers on their sides to allow the stems to drop away more easily. Do not force the last piece of stem from the tuber, as this will only cause damage. Have patience, for it will eventually drop off. (An exception may be tubers from cuttings where the short stem remains firmly attached to the tuber. In this case, leaving it, especially if the tuber is small, will assist with wintering over.)

When all the foliage has fallen away, there is no rush to remove the tuber. It is preferable to let the mix dry out thoroughly. This may take some weeks.

Some growers leave the tubers in their containers right through the winter months, provided they have sufficient space to store them that way. However, I do not advocate this method, as it is not possible to inspect each tuber on a regular basis throughout the winter. Infestation by the vine weevil grub (a worldwide pest) will result in its being entirely eaten away by the following spring. Also, the scab, which forms over the wound left by the stem, cannot be removed, and this may cause the tuber to rot.

'Harbridge Peach'

Tubers resulting from cuttings taken earlier in the season tend not to be particularly large and are an exception to this. If they are stored in the normal manner over winter, they tend to dry out and often shrivel up to nothing. However, if left undisturbed in the dry mix in their container with their roots still attached, they are more likely to maintain good condition. They should never be watered during storage.

Cleaning and storing tubers

It is very important that good care be taken to avoid heavy losses over the winter months to ensure another season's vibrant display. I personally recommend the following system.

Allow the mix in the containers to dry out thoroughly. Do not attempt to remove and clean the tuber before this has occurred. When the mix is really dry, knock out the tuber and gently break the mix and roots away, taking great care not to damage the tuber's skin, as any area of damaged skin will not produce roots in the future. A soft brush is ideal for this. Any rot should be cut out and the area dusted with flowers of sulfate or other anti-fungal powder. The tubers should then have their labels affixed with a NEW elastic band (old bands deteriorate and break) and be set in the sun and air to complete the drying process.

Tubers may be stored either loose or in some form of medium, although I store my mature tubers without any medium whatsoever in shallow, open containers. By not overcrowding and leaving plenty of space between each tuber, I find that, should any rot, the remainder stay disease-free. I always dust the whole box with an insecticide and anti-fungal powder as a preventive measure. The storage area

Above left: 'Avalanche'
Above right: 'Sweet Dreams'

must be well-ventilated, and the boxes need sufficient holes to allow air movement when they are stacked. It is necessary that the storage area, although cool, be frost-free. I store my trays in my brick garage where the temperature can drop to 32°F (0°C) but where they are safe from frost damage. In very cold zones, an unheated cellar or attic, provided the temperature does not drop below freezing, is suitable for storage. In very hot climates, an insulated container will keep the temperature constant and ensure a period of dormancy.

Some growers prefer to store tubers in some type of medium, keeping air from them and thus preventing shrinkage. The medium must be completely dry; otherwise, the result will be mold and rot. Pumice, vermiculite or perlite is suitable, whereas old potting mix or sawdust should be treated with caution. Inspection of the tubers is made more difficult with this method of storage. Tubers should be checked at least once every month for any sign of rot or weevils. Early detection can mean the difference between saving the tuber and its total loss.

Removal of scabs

At the first inspection, remove the scabs that have formed over the wounds where stems joined tubers, because rot is more likely to start under unremoved scabs.

Insert the point of a sharp, stiff knife under the edge of the scab before flicking it off. Dust the exposed clean flesh with sulfur or other anti-fungal powder. If the scab does not come away easily, then give it more time to dry before trying again.

CHAPTER 6

Basket Begonias

Generally, basket or Pendula begonias have smaller flowers than their upright cousins—but what they lack in size they make up for by the sheer number of blooms they produce. A good display of hanging basket plants is a joy to behold and the color range today is extensive.

The actual methods of growing and care are very similar to those described in the last chapter for the Large-flowered Tuberhybrida, although finding a suitably protected place to grow them may be a little more difficult. While named uprights also need protection, baskets hung high are more vulnerable and can be destroyed in a matter of minutes in a high wind.

A wire basket lined with moss holds this cream pendula.

Starting
Starting basket begonias is no different from starting uprights, but the method used will depend on individual circumstances. If bottom heat is available, it will be possible to get the plants into flower much earlier.

If no heated facilities are available, or there is insufficient heated space at the start of the season, then a different approach is necessary. For the most part, I move my Pendula tubers from their cold winter environment into a warm one, as I do the Large-flowered varieties, to encourage budding up. However, when good buds are in evidence, the tubers are potted directly into appropriately-sized baskets, covered with mix and watered, using the same open, free-draining potting mix as for all my

other plants. Although they may be moved outside as soon as the danger of frost is past, good growth will occur only when the daytime temperature is 55°F (13°C).

My main outdoor area is roofed, so I can hang most containers directly on the hook on which they will spend the summer months, since the containers will not become waterlogged with spring rains. If the available area is not roofed, the baskets should be placed somewhere protected from the rain—preferably a warm, sunny location. Watering must be sparse until a good root system is evident.

Containers for basket begonias
There are really only two choices of conventional containers for basket begonias—wire baskets or those made of plastic, both of which come in various sizes and shapes. But, in effect, the choice is limited only by the grower's imagination. I have seen

Opposite: A colorful display of baskets and plants under a roofed area.

Examples of containers for begonias: (above) a plastic basket; (right) coconut lining in a wire basket; (opposite) wall-mounted half-baskets.

effective displays in a wide range of unusual objects, including up-ended drainpipes and hollowed-out logs.

Wire baskets require lining to contain the potting mix. A number of materials are available, such as sphagnum moss, coconut fiber, or a type of felt. Sphagnum moss is probably the most popular despite its cost, and a basket made with fresh moss does look very attractive. The moss can be used from year to year, although it often needs to be added to because of shrinkage. Sphagnum comes in both a loose form and in compressed, pre-cut shapes, but the latter is a much more expensive option. (The use of sphagnum is causing some concern within environmental groups and there are now synthetic alternatives that are also attractive and reusable.) Coconut and felt liners come in pre-cut shapes, ready to place inside the basket.

Half-baskets, sometimes known as manger baskets, are also available and are ideal for use on walls and fences; in addition, quarter-baskets can be useful for filling corners.

A wire basket with moss can be very heavy to lift, especially after watering. I use 16 in (40 cm) wire baskets for my very large tubers—one to each container—but try to avoid moving them once they are planted up and in their final position.

Plastic baskets come in various shapes and sizes. In the main, I use the same size for all my Pendulas, namely the 12 in (30 cm) round type. If the tubers are small, I place three to such a container, but only one when tubers are larger, say, 2 in (5 cm) or more in diameter. If small tubers are planted individually, they will need a smaller container.

The containers I use have a rolled down lip, which gives them added strength, and they can be used with either a chain or plastic hanger. The plastic hangers are cheaper than the chain hangers and make it easier to lift the container down, as, with a hand underneath, the container can be lifted off the hook. However, they tend to weaken over time, especially when placed in sunlight, leading to a disaster should they break, whereas chains have a longer life. In the end, the choice is a matter of personal preference.

Babylon containers come with both a saucer and a grill, the latter being inserted inside about 1 in (2.5 cm) above the bottom of the container. This prevents the mix from touching the water, which will lie in the saucer and the bottom of the container, but at the same time will allow the plant roots to pass through and reach the water. While saucers alone can cause the mix to remain soggy and become sour, a grill such as this overcomes the problem and even becomes an advantage, giving the plant a reserve of water on hot days. If watering is done judiciously, the saucer will also prevent baskets from dripping on other plants growing below. If Babylon containers are unavailable, there are other self-watering pots available that will work equally well.

Location

An ideal situation for your begonias is one sheltered from the wind, hot sun and rain. If your baskets are in a conservatory or greenhouse, the elements won't be a problem, except perhaps for hot sun. I am fortunate enough to have an area measuring 54 x 6 ft (16 x 2 m) running the full length of my house, roofed with transparent corrugated plastic. This area is on the sunny side and therefore gets plenty of light. I have reduced the amount of wind by dropping a piece of shadecloth vertically from the outside edge of the roof to the level of the base of the baskets (see photograph, page 42).

Without such a roof, rain can be a problem, not only because of direct damage to the flowers, but also because the added weight to a branch in full flower may result in it breaking off. A cheaper alternative to the more effective transparent roof, and one that will minimize damage, is a shelter of shadecloth. This breaks up the raindrops into a gentle mist, although it may not totally prevent breakages.

When placing hooks on the roof of the protected area, remember that a well-grown basket may measure up to 3 ft (90 cm) across. It is easier to allow space at the outset, rather than to struggle to move heavy baskets later because they are banging into each other and damaging the flowers. Also, make sure the hooks are strong enough to support

the weight of the fully-grown plant.

An alternative, attractive location for baskets is hanging from low branches of trees, where the leaves afford protection from both rain and hot sun.

Improving the display

In contrast to the standard begonias, all the growing shoots are left on a hanging plant. When it is growing well, and the stems are between 6–8 in (15–20 cm) long, all flower buds and the growing tip of each stem should be pinched out, as should the tips of any side shoots. This forces the shoots to branch out and consequently produce more flowers. The process can be repeated if desired, although it will delay flowering by two to three weeks each time. While not essential, this procedure does make a dif-

Shadecloth protects the hanging baskets that provide a focal point in this garden.

Above: 'Michelle'
Left: A ruffled begonia from Antonelli Brothers.

Watering

Pendula begonias, particularly those in wire baskets, tend to dry out more rapidly than the standard varieties, since they are more exposed and have far greater air movement around them. In warmer areas or if drying out becomes a problem, water-retentive crystals and gels are available which can be mixed into the potting medium to act as a reservoir of water. Instructions for use are on the packaging.

Other cultural details

Other details for the care of baskets, such as feeding, end-of-season wind-down, cleaning and storage, are essentially the same as for their upright cousins (see pages 47–51). Once the plant is flowering, care is relatively trouble-free. They do not need staking, and the flowers do not need supporting.

ference to the final display. I find that, with over 100 baskets, I have the time to do it only once, but even this once is well worthwhile.

Unlike the upright begonias, with basket plantings it is not the size of the individual bloom that matters most, but the overall mass of flowers produced. Thus, with Pendulas, for greater effect all the flowers are left on, whether male or female.

CHAPTER 7

Begonias in the Garden

Given a suitable situation, tuberous begonias do well in the garden. This applies even in cold zones, though for a shorter part of the year. Particularly popular are the smaller Non-stop and Multiflora types, but even some of the Large-flowered varieties will thrive. I use the garden to trial my first-year Large-flowered seedlings raised from my previous year's hybridizing, which gives me the benefit of an attractive garden display, while assessing their worth before deciding if any are good enough for future promotion to a container.

Choice of site

During the hotter part of the day, some shade, such as that afforded by a large tree or fence, is desirable. However, if hardened off by gradual exposure to the sun, tuberous begonias can tolerate a fair amount of sunshine, though excess heat will burn the fleshy leaves. Generally, the Non-stops and Multifloras are more tolerant of the heat and sun.

Preparing the ground

The ground should be prepared as for any other garden plant. Just before planting, when danger of frost is past, broadcast a good general fertilizer evenly over the area to be planted and then fork it in lightly. Half a teaspoonful of controlled-release fertilizer may be placed into the base of the hole made for each plant.

Planting

Plants should be set in the ground with the points of the leaves facing the direction the flowers are to face. This is easy to work out with seedlings, but

Above: A garden trial plot for first-year Large-flowered hybrid seedlings.
Opposite: Apricot Multifloras provide a colorful border for this garden path

budded-up tubers may have been planted before they had any top growth, so when the foliage forms, some of the plants may not be facing the right way. In this case, lift the whole plant, taking a good clump of earth, and turn it to the desired position.

Good spacing of at least 8 in (20 cm) between

the plants should be allowed to ensure good air movement, helping to prevent the onset of disease.

In areas where the soil temperature warms only slowly in the spring, the tubers may be placed into containers or trays at the budded-up stage, and started as described for the Large-flowered varieties (see page 42). The smaller dirt mass will warm relatively quickly, especially when the containers are placed in a sheltered, sunny position. The plants are ready for the garden when they are 3–4 in (7–10 cm) high, with roots showing on the edge of the mix when knocked out of their containers. Because they have a good root system, they never look back and will flower some weeks earlier than if planted directly into the cold garden soil as budded-up tubers.

A useful option with both seedlings and tubers destined for the garden is to use lattice pots with slots cut down the sides, which are available from hydroponic suppliers. The roots are able to find their way through the slots and make use of the nutrients in the soil. At the end of the season, it makes lifting the plants and finding the tubers easy.

Staking

Multiflora and small Non-stops do not require additional support, and all shoots and flowers should be left on. However, if the Large-flowered types are grown in the garden, they normally require some staking and tying as they grow, both to prevent wind damage and to enhance the effect. With these, as with the container-grown plants, removal of surplus shoots will improve flower size and plant shape, but the female flowers may be left on to give more color.

Watering

Overhead watering, like rain, tends to damage the blooms. It is preferable to use a trickle or ground-soaking method so the flowers will not be spoiled by the water. This also reduces the chance of disease. Of course, we have no control over the weather and plants in the open garden will naturally get wet

when it rains, but watering from below minimizes such problems.

End of the season

When the plants start to go yellow and disintegrate with the onset of fall, consider lifting the tubers from the garden. This is essential only where the ground freezes, but, as with the other types of tuberous begonias, it is a good policy.

If the tubers were planted directly into the ground, dig them up when the foliage has fallen away—usually the first frost will fix this—and remove any excess soil. Then place the tubers in boxes or trays and put them in a dry location until the remaining soil dries and can be easily removed.

Above: A garden display featuring Multifloras makes an arresting display.
Left: Multiflora and Non-stop begonias create a vibrant effect in a small garden bed.

Subsequent cleaning and care has already been described (see page 50).

If a lattice pot has been used, this process is easier. Lift the pot, along with any top foliage. Remove any excess roots outside the container and place the plants somewhere to dry off. They require no further water, and the top growth falls away naturally.

Other cultural details are the same as for container culture of Large-flowered tuberous varieties (see Chapter 5).

CHAPTER 8

Pests, Diseases and Disorders

Few pests or diseases trouble begonias. Most can be guarded against by paying attention to the basic requirements of ventilation and humidity. If you choose to use chemical controls, manufacturer's instructions should be carefully observed, including the use of protective clothing.

Main pests
Vine weevil
The black vine weevil (*Otiorhynchus sulcatus*) is found throughout the world and in some areas causes severe damage to commercial crops. With the increased use of container plants, it has spread from nurseries and now flourishes in our gardens.

Adult weevils are about $^1/_2$ in (1 cm) long and black, with a number of lighter spots on the shell. The first adults emerge in early spring and continue to do so over a period of about two months. Although they are flightless, they are evidently excellent climbers, as larvae are often found in tubers of Pendula begonias hanging many feet above the ground.

The larvae, which are legless, are about $^1/_4$ in (7 mm) in length. They are crescent-shaped, white or cream in color, with a light brown head. Pupation occurs in mid- to late winter in a smooth-walled cell in a tuber, in the potting mix, or in open ground.

The weevils enjoy a varied diet, with the adults feeding at night on the leaves of any of some 100 different plants, where they leave a characteristic notched pattern on the edges. But the larvae are the most destructive during late summer and fall, with their unobserved voracious attack on the roots and, in the case of begonias, on the tubers. The growing plant, under attack by these larvae, may wilt and not thrive, as the small roots so important to growth are being eaten.

It pays to check a wilting plant for any signs of infestation by knocking it out to check the roots rather than applying more water immediately. A dormant tuber infested by the weevil larvae may have anything from one small hole to many holes, or may even be just a husk where the weevils have dined out in style.

The most sensible way to combat all pests and diseases is with prevention, and this is particularly so with the vine weevil, since most controls are very toxic.

Avoid growing begonias with plants such as cyclamen, which have a reputation as one of the weevils' favorite foods. Check the root ball of any growing Tuberhybrida purchased or received during the season, and be vigilant for evidence of activity when repotting tubers. Potential hiding places, such as plant debris and loose boards, are best kept clear of the begonia growing area. It may be possible to

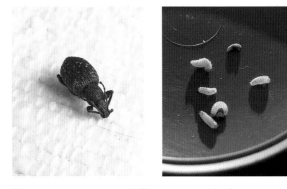

The vine weevil beetle (left) and grubs (right).

Spacing plants to aid air flow helps to prevent disease.

catch the adults by looking in such places (or setting a board down as a trap), but they are shy and nocturnal, so a flashlight search is the only way to find them.

Careful cleaning and inspection of lifted dormant tubers, with perhaps a dip in insecticide, will prevent the weevil larvae transferring from one tuber to the others in their storage area. When potting, fresh mix from a reputable source is recommended; the re-use of old potting mix should be avoided. As few as six larvae in a container can produce 6000 offspring in a season—thus, even one left in old mix can lead to problems.

Most controls are intended for attacking the larvae and are mixed with potting mixes or in the soil to give protection throughout the growing season. The active ingredient in such products is chlorpyrifos, a contact and ingested organophosphorus—be warned that these are toxic chemicals,

and any leftover mix cannot be used on the vegetable garden.

Less toxic are the liquid chemicals that contain the active ingredient oxamyl, a systemic carbamoyloxime insecticide, such as Vydate. Alternatively, liquid Diazinon, a contact organophosphorus insecticide, is very effective. Such products should be watered into the mix or soil in the form of a drench and will kill any larvae. This treatment should be repeated at least three times during the growing season, timed to coincide with peak larval activity (August, September and October) and is, in my opinion, the most effective way of controlling this pest.

Biological controls are also available in the form of nematodes. These microscopic creatures enter the bodies of the larvae, kill them, and continue to multiply, killing any new grubs that hatch during the growing season. The downside is their very short shelf-life and the large quantities they are marketed in, making it difficult for the home gardener to use them.

It is possible that some of these products may soon be withdrawn from the market given the concern of the effect on the environment of these toxic substances. This makes the preventative measures that have been described, and the biological controls an even more attractive option.

Mites

There are a number of different types of mite, some clearly visible with the naked eye, such as the European red mite, and others visible only with a microscope, such as the Tarsonemid or cyclamen mite. The latter are the most common type found on begonias. Consequently, their presence may not be noted until after the damage to the buds and growth tips, where they live, has occurred.

Symptoms of a mite infestation are a cork-like substance on the stems of plants and the underside

A shriveled begonia bud shows the devastating effect of mite damage.

of leaves. The growing tips turn brown and become very brittle, collapsing when touched. Flower buds become distorted, and a brown stain is seen as the flower struggles to open. Plants can be decimated in a very short space of time, and the mites are often well-established before the symptoms are readily apparent.

Mites thrive in hot, dry conditions, so growing under glass heightens the risk of an infestation. Both high humidity and good ventilation around the plants will help prevent infection. Other plants known to be sources of mites should not be grown in the vicinity of begonias; these include cyclamen and strawberries. A wise preventive measure is to isolate new acquisitions, regardless of the source. I go further and spray them at weekly intervals for three weeks before allowing them to join my stock.

Note that insecticides are not effective against mites, and a proper miticide (acaricide) is required. Generally, the more lethal to mites, the more toxic the spray, so take full precautions when using the sprays. Application rates and instructions are recorded on the containers.

Low-toxicity sprays may prove effective, perhaps largely because of the mites' dislike of moisture. Seaweed products, which can also be applied as a foliar feed, keep the pests at bay, possibly because of the smell. Pest oil and wettable sulfur are other low-toxicity methods and, again, will have the application rates and instructions recorded on the containers. Another non-toxic option is washing soda (sodium carbonate), using 1 teaspoon in 2 gallons (9 L) of cold water, plus a squirt of detergent. Plants can either be sprayed with this solution or totally immersed, if not too large.

Minor pests

Some other pests that may occasionally occur are root mealybugs, thrips, the green looper caterpillar and sciarid flies (peat gnats). These can generally be readily controlled with the use of any good insecticide.

Main diseases
Mildew
Powdery mildew is a fungal disease that attacks a wide variety of ornamental plants, including all begonias. The damage due to infection by the fungi can be slight to severe; affect some plants and not others; and be worse in some seasons than in others.

Usually the first symptoms of the disease are white to pale gray fungus growths—similar to small white stars—which appear on the leaves, stems or flowers. Young plants and those under any stress, such as one that is badly in need of water, tend to be the first affected and more severely damaged than older, healthy ones.

Generally speaking, mildew is more prevalent in the fall when high humidity is rapidly converted to moisture by the onset of cooler evenings. Moisture allows the spores to germinate. In a conservatory or greenhouse, adequate air circulation is vital, as is control of the humidity. Shadehouses have the advantage of better ventilation, but jamming plants close together will be counterproductive, as it will reduce the all-important airflow around them. In the open garden, good spacing will reduce the chances of infection. Spraying and watering is best done in the early morning, with care taken not to wet the foliage when watering.

Wise plant selection may be helpful for the grower who has particular trouble with mildew, since some begonias are more susceptible than others. Examples of these include *Begonia sutherlandii, B. gracilis* var *martiana*, and *B. dregei* among the species, and 'Avalanche' and 'Lou Anne' among the tuberous hybrids. On the other hand, many begonias seem to be immune to this disease, even when grown among infected plants.

An option in areas particularly mildew-prone is to consider adopting a preventive spray program from the beginning of the season. Many different fungicides, some of which are systemic, are available in different locations. Before buying the spray, check the information given on the container for

Mildew on a begonia leaf.

the following names, as these are the present-day chemicals supposedly best suited to controlling powdery mildew: proaconazole, myclobutanil, triforine, tridemorph, penconazole and fenarimol. In some instances, copper fungicides can also be effective. Sulfur, both as a spray or a dust, is also effective and is now available as a soluble powder. As opposed to all other sprays, mildew does not become resistant to sulfur.

One old remedy, for those who prefer not to use toxic sprays, is to use 2 tablespoons of baking soda to 1 gallon (4 L) of water applied as a spray. Another natural product one can use is milk. In an experiment carried out in South America, it was found that milk diluted with ten parts of clean water and sprayed once a week was very effective in controlling powdery mildew on vegetables. A number of amateur growers I know, who have had mildew problems, have used this remedy and claim success.

Botrytis (stem rot or brown rot)
Botrytis is a fungal disease that can attack any part of a begonia plant, particularly in the latter part of the season, as does mildew, since it is associated

Above: Treating botrytis on a plant stem (left) by removing the affected area (center, note the healthy stem beneath), and dusting the stem with sulfur (right).

with the same conditions that favor the development of mildew. Botrytis is evidenced by the appearance of a wet, soggy, brownish area which, if left untreated, will quickly increase in size and may eventually kill the plant. In the tuber, botrytis usually results from damage or failure to remove the scab. Another form of botrytis that affects tubers in storage is dry rot, when they go hard for no apparent reason and die.

Botrytis usually affects plants, or parts of plants, that have either been damaged or have insufficient ventilation, or where the grower's hygiene is poor. Examples are a tie cutting into the stem of the plant, or the plants being too close together, or falling flowers becoming lodged in the foliage below. Excess nitrogen will also predispose a growing plant to botrytis because the new growth is soft.

Again, good hygiene, adequate ventilation, and plant spacing are of paramount importance in preventing the onset of botrytis. Pay particular attention to removing stems and leaves as they drop, for they will cause the infection to start, when left lying on other parts of the plant.

If any area of rot is found, it must be dealt with immediately, especially if it is close to the tuber.

The first step is to clean a knife or scalpel by dipping it in methylated spirits. If the stem is rotten right through, then the only option is to cut it off cleanly with the sterilized knife below the infection, which may mean the end of that particular plant's growth for the season. If the stem is only partly infected, then the area can be cut away carefully, ensuring that all the rot is removed. The cutting instrument should be cleaned both during and after use. Once all the rot is removed, wash the wound with methylated spirits, which will both sterilize and dry it. Then dust the wound with either flowers of sulfate or another anti-fungal powder. This will have the dual effect of drying off the wound and sealing it from possible further infection.

The removal of a portion of the stem may weaken it to the point where it can no longer support itself, and further staking may be required. If the required surgery leaves just a short stump protruding above the mix in the container, then be careful when watering this plant. At the later stage of the season (October), I would lay the plant on its side on a shelf and allow it to dry out slowly, leaving the piece of stem to fall off naturally. Further watering at this stage will very likely lead to rot in the tuber. If the surgery is necessary much earlier in the season, then a small amount of water will be required to keep the tuber going, in which case it may well send up shoots again.

Disorders

Blindness

Occasionally a plant may suddenly go "blind". In effect, the growing tip of the plant ceases to exist, and the plant can no longer grow upward and hence does not produce flowers. This phenomenon is not caused by any pest or disease and usually rights itself the following season. Any cuttings taken from such a plant do not, in my experience, copy this trait. Sometimes the plant in question has a side shoot lower down, in which case this shoot may be trained to take over the role of the main stem, and the plant will flower normally, although a little late.

Foliar petal

Foliar petal is a condition where green, leaf-like petals replace the actual dorsal or guard petal of the flower buds, giving the appearance of a leaf rather than the normal petal. This often happens on the first few buds of the season, with subsequent flowers being normal, and is more prevalent on the paler white and yellow varieties. The condition is not caused by any pest or disease but is thought to result from overfeeding—particularly with nitrogen—in the early stages of the plant's growth, although there is no scientific evidence that this is so. Any affected buds should be removed.

Corky scab (edema)

This condition gives the appearance of a pale brown, cork-like scale on the plant stems and the underside of young leaves. It should not be confused with marking left by mites—corky scab is coarser and covers areas rather than appearing in the form of lines. The cause is often overpotting. When a young plant is overpotted, its small root system is unable to cope with the amount of moisture available in the mix. The leaves try their best to transpire this moisture, but there is so much that their cell structures burst, leaving the brown corklike appearance. In turn, since the plant can now cope with even less moisture because of the damaged leaf

A begonia flower with foliar petal.

cells, the soil becomes even more waterlogged, resulting in the actual drowning of the roots. No oxygen is able to get into the mix, which in turn reduces the plant's ability to function. If continuously exposed to excess moisture, the roots will rot, causing the plant to die.

Bud drop

The dropping of buds as they form may occur if the plant is under some form of stress, such as excessively high temperatures, especially if accompanied by low humidity. Overwatering or rapid changes of temperature are other causes. Large-flowered Tuberhybrida can make difficult houseplants because of the lack of both ventilation and humidity, so bud drop is common when plants are taken indoors for more than a day or two at a time. Outside, bud drop is not so prevalent, although it will occur in hot, dry conditions. Every effort must be made to keep the humidity high, with pebble trays filled with water or humidifiers in conservatories, or by wetting the floor in the shadehouse or greenhouse in the morning or early afternoon.

CHAPTER 9

Fertilizers and Soils

NPK

The letters NPK represent the three main nutrient compounds of a fertilizer. N stands for nitrogen, essential for cell extension, protein building and photosynthesis, i.e., plant growth; P is for phosphorus, which plants need for photosynthesis, the development of roots and the production of flowers; and K is for potassium (potash), which protects from disease and improves the color of flowers.

Fertilizers, when added to a growing medium, supply nutrients (NPK and other trace elements) essential for the health and growth of the plant. There are two main types: organic fertilizers, which are derived from plant and animal remains and often referred to as manures; and inorganic, which are manmade and manufactured by chemical processes.

Organic fertilizers help improve the physical condition of the soil by the addition of humus and micro-organisms. The nutrient content will vary enormously, depending on the source of the manure. Inorganic fertilizers provide nutrients that are usually water soluble and therefore quickly available. They are in higher concentrations of NPK and are able to be applied in measured doses.

A complete fertilizer will contain these three major nutrients, and the relative proportions should be stated on the container. Flowering plants like begonias need a relatively high proportion of potassium (K) to that of nitrogen, otherwise fleshy growth and small flowers will result. This may be

Opposite: The right potting mix and nutrition will ensure beautiful results, like this white-red picotee.

qualified slightly in that, early in the begonia season, before flowering, a fertilizer with a somewhat higher proportion of nitrogen (N) is desirable to get good plant growth established.

In addition to these three main nutrients, there are numerous others (micronutrients or trace elements), as plants need a balanced amount of at least 16 of these for healthy growth. A large number of them come from carbon dioxide in the air, water, and from the solids that comprise the growing medium.

Slow-release vs standard fertilizers

In the past, a base fertilizer was added to the mix and liquid feed was used during the season. This is certainly the direct, hands-on approach and one that arguably gives more control to increase, reduce or change the nutrients given to the plants. The result of such an approach, though more demanding and troublesome, should be better plants and flowers. At the level of serious competitive showing, this method may be preferred.

A relatively recent introduction in the world of horticulture is the slow-release type of fertilizers, which has eased the burden of working out a balanced feeding program. A number of these products are on the market, with the proportion of ingredients varied according to intended use, e.g., for shrubs, container plants or bulbs. In addition, the duration of their effectiveness can vary considerably, some being designed to release their nutrients in just three months and others for up to two years. Some also contain the trace elements essential to plant health. Although virtually foolproof, excess use of these products, as with any other fertilizer, will result in problems with the plants, so always refer to the manufacturer's directions.

My preference now is to rely for the full growing season entirely on the slow-release fertilizer added to the mix, one that has added trace elements and is designed to last a minimum of six months. And the results are excellent. This way, I believe I can be sure of just what the plants are getting. I do give a little assistance to the plant once it has become established in its first container with a foliar feed sprayed onto the plant. This assists in the production of a good, effective root system on which the plant depends for its energy and growth.

Foliar feeding can be done two to three times per week, but must be stopped when no further flower buds are to be removed. Failure to do so will result in damage to the buds and resulting flowers. Spraying in full sun should be avoided, as scorching of the leaves will result.

A recipe for foliar feed
Urea: 20 oz (500 g)
Nitrate of Potash: 20 oz (500 g)
Epsom Salts: 4 oz (100 g)
Dissolve the above in 9 pints (4.5 L) of water, to give a concentrated stock solution. About 2 tablespoons (50 ml) of this solution in ½ gallon (2 L) of water is then used as a spray.

An alternative method is to water in extra food once a week along with normal watering. In this case, a high-potash fertilizer is recommended. Schultz, an American brand, can be purchased in various forms, allowing the matching of the NPK proportions to individual requirements. Always avoid giving fertilizer to dry plants, for this may cause root burn.

A healthy plant grown in a soilless growing medium, using only the slow-release fertilizer present in the original mix.

Potting mix

In the days before bagged mixes were readily available, there were many and varied recipes for the "right" potting medium for tuberous begonias. Even today, when a suitable ready-made mix may generally be purchased from the local nursery, some people prefer to mix their own, and debate can still get heated among enthusiasts on the respective merits of various recipes.

A primary requirement of a good mix for begonias is that it is open and free-draining. It is essential that water, as it drains from any mix, is replaced in the tiny spaces by oxygen. Oxygen is an essential ingredient to the life of any plant. It is necessary also that the particles of the mix are able to retain moisture, another essential requirement for healthy plants. Finally, the mix should contain a balanced

supply of nutrients and be free of disease-causing organisms.

In the past, loam-based mixes were used for begonias. These generally consisted of topsoil (including grass and roots to a depth of about 2 in/ 5 cm) and cow manure rotted in layers for a year or more to make loam, and then put through a coarse mesh, before mixing with peat, grit (to improve drainage) and fertilizers. These loam mixes were relatively heavy and slow to drain. Judging the watering requirements necessary for container culture left little margin for error and was the downfall of many growers, even though clay containers, which allow greater evaporation, were used.

The introduction and popularity of plastic containers with lower evaporation levels made watering even more difficult when using such mixes. Further-

more, good loam has become much harder to find. Labor costs have also played a big part in the demise of commercial production. Nevertheless, a few growers still prefer loam-based mixes and, provided they have a good understanding of the different approach to watering, achieve good results.

Today most mixes are soilless, made from a combination of various ingredients, most commonly with peat as the basis and substances added to improve drainage. However, peat is a non-renewable resource.

Making your own mix

Do not be put off by the thought of mixing your own, as it is not necessary to make large amounts. The smaller the amount of finished mix, however, the more important it is that the ingredients are added in the correct proportions. If you have a good recipe, follow it to the letter.

Purchasing ready-made mix

It should be possible to select a commercial mix with details on the bag of the composition, the date the contents were mixed and bagged, the type of fertilizer that has been added, whether it will last for three, four, five or six months and, most importantly, the pH of the mix. Unfortunately, regulations do not exist in all countries requiring such listings, and even where they do, a formula is not required, simply a list of the contents. Thus, the purchase of pre-made mix can be chancy.

Most potting mixes contain controlled-release fertilizer. These pellets of fertilizer begin their work when they come into contact with moisture and heat. If, at the time of purchase, the product is three to four months old—and this is not uncommon—a large proportion of the nutrients will already have been released as the coatings on the fertilizer pellets start to break down. This means that the contents of the bag may actually be detrimental to the plants, due to the build-up of the nutrient salts that may burn the young roots, causing stunted growth and eventually tuber rot.

A dual-purpose pH and moisture meter.

So it makes sense to try and find a nursery or landscape firm that actually makes potting mix and can confirm that the product is fresh. If a check of the pH level shows it is not correct, at least someone can rectify the problem. Better still is to have such a firm make up a mix to a specific recipe, although there is usually a minimum requirement, which is generally a quantity that is far more than most people require. Ideally, try and source a mix specifically designed for begonias.

What is pH?

The pH scale is a measurement of a soil's sweetness or sourness. Sweet soils are alkaline and sour ones are acidic. The scale ranges from 1 to 14, with 1 being acidic, 7 neutral, and 14 alkaline. Most soils range between 5 and 8.

The significance of this is that the optimal release of the building blocks of plant growth, health and flowering, i.e., nitrogen, phosphorous and potassium, occurs within this narrow range of pH values.

Plants growing in a medium with a pH range between 5 and 8 have most nutrients available to them. However, if the reading is below 5.5 or above 7.5, then problems begin to occur, preventing the uptake of essential trace elements by the plant. Begonias favor a slightly acidic medium, with a pH between 6.3 and 6.8, for optimal performance.

The pH may be measured using soil test kits or soil probes, which are available quite cheaply from garden centers. Although they are not scientifically accurate, they are close enough to give a fair indication. Electronic meters are more accurate, but they are considerably more expensive.

As an alternative, the mix/soil may be tested scientifically by a soil-testing laboratory that offers this test as well as a full soil analysis.

Adjusting for imbalance

It pays to check the pH of the growing medium in the latter part of the season, particularly if a lot of water has been applied. If the mix/soil has become too acidic, correct it by watering in a top-dressing of lime (calcium carbonate). If the pH errs on the alkaline side, it may be corrected by the addition of sulfur or iron sulfate. In either case, caution should prevail, as a very small amount can make a large difference.

A balanced decision

In summary, the choice of growing medium must be balanced with choice of container and watering style.

Plastic containers require a more open mix than clay containers of a similar size, and squat containers need a more open mix than tall ones. Plastic containers lose moisture only from the exposed surface of the mix, while clay containers breathe and allow moisture to evaporate through the walls. Using a fine mix, especially a soil-based one, in plastic containers will result in the "fines" washing to the bottom, preventing drainage and keeping the mix in the container too wet. This, in turn, will prevent oxygen from entering, which leads to root rot. On the other hand, clay containers containing an open mix may dry out too rapidly.

Watering plants in soil-based mixes requires fine judgment and will sometimes be necessary only once a week or less. It is harder to kill plants with open, free-draining mixes, making them a more suitable choice for the novice grower.

CHAPTER 10

Watering

As with humans, more than 90 percent of the gross weight of plants is water, so it is essential that a correct balance be maintained to ensure good plant health and quality. Water is essential for plant respiration, photosynthesis and the general metabolism of plants. It is also an active diluent of unwanted products. One of the first signs of insufficient water is the lack of turgidity in the foliage and stems, which, if ignored, progresses to leaf scorching and finally the death of the plant. Nevertheless, though our plants die without this essential element, more plants—especially houseplants—are killed through overwatering than underwatering.

Water quality

Water quality is very important. Contamination, such as with spray residues, will cause problems, as will hard water in areas where the catchment is in a limestone region. Deposits may be left on plant leaves following watering or spraying. More damaging, however, is the buildup of calcium, which will raise the pH level of the potting mix over the season. If this occurs, the plants will not be able to take up sufficient quantities of trace elements or phosphorus (see pH for corrective measures). To prevent these problems, collect and use rainwater, which is extremely soft. It will also be pure, unless a source of pollution affects the collection roof.

Deciding when to water

A plant's need for water is a matter of the individual grower's personal judgment and experience. Watering requirements depend on many things: the size of the plant, the number of flowers it is carrying,

Hand-watering can become quite a chore if you have a lot of hanging baskets.

the size and type of container used (clay, plastic or moss-lined basket), the type of mix, the temperature and the wind. A useful check is to pick up the container. If it is light, then it is dry; if not, no harm will result from leaving watering for another day. A moisture meter is a handy accessory.

Begonias thrive on being allowed to dry out a little before further water is added, because plants require oxygen as well as water to perform well. When the plants dry out a little, oxygen is drawn down into the spaces left in the mix as the water either drains out or is used by the plant.

When possible, it is good practice to water plants in the morning to diminish the risk of fungal disease. At all times, it is preferable not to get water on the flowers and foliage, since the flowers will damage easily, and wet foliage will burn if touched by the rays of the sun.

Watering methods

Personally, I do not think it is possible to improve on hand-watering. It ensures that individual attention can be given to each plant, which must be advantageous, given differing individual requirements. Having said that, I still believe there are good reasons for having an automatic watering system.

Watering a few containers or baskets of begonias is not a difficult task. If one wishes to go away for a few days, or in the event of illness, friends, neighbors or relatives may offer to help. But, despite specific instructions, plants are often overwatered, resulting in serious problems. For this reason, some growers will not leave their plants during the season.

For growers with a large number of plants, hand-watering becomes a daily chore taking several hours. I have chosen to use an automatic system to do the bulk of my watering. In the early part of the season, though, all my plants are hand-watered, since plants at different stages of growth require differing amounts of water—difficult to achieve automatically. I like to keep my young plants quite dry to encourage good root growth, and therefore prefer a hands-on approach. When they are all growing well in the final containers, which are all the same size, I transfer them to the automatic system.

Later in the season I may supplement the watering of individual plants by hand, despite daily automatic watering. I do this as I take each plant from its display to work on it, e.g., for ties and supports. If I feel it needs additional water, then I give it some by hand.

Automatic systems

The most basic automatic system consists of a manual timer attached to the water source. Although inexpensive, such timers are of limited value, since the water still has to be turned on each day. All they do is turn the water off. However, they do give control over the amount of water the plants receive.

Programmable, battery-operated timers are limited to watering one "station" or area only, unless an expensive attachment is fitted. The timer is placed in the water line between the water source and the plants. It operates by opening a mechanical valve, allowing the water to flow into the piping system and closing it off after the set time has elapsed. These timers are easy to install and program and can be set to water up to four times in one day if required. One set of small AA batteries will generally last the whole summer. They are ideal for large collections, a shadehouse or a greenhouse, or a display of baskets, and can easily cope with up to 100 containers, providing the water pressure is sufficient.

More sophisticated still are the electronic timers, most of which operate off the main circuit through a transformer, generally supplied in the price. These reduce the power to a safe level, e.g., 6, 12, or 24 volts. The waterproof models have the transformer enclosed, while the others come as a separate item and require installation in a weatherproof area. Electronic timers may control six, eight, ten, or even 12 stations. Each station, or area, to control needs a solenoid valve, an additional cost. These solenoids are placed in the water line close to the source for the area. A wire then runs from each solenoid back to the timer, and the electrical impulse it sends out opens and closes the valve according to the setting. They are very simple to install and do not require an electrician. The prices vary according to their complexity, and there are many on the market.

Whatever the type of timer used, plastic piping must be run from the water source to the plants. Needs vary according to distance and water pressure, e.g., where I live, I have found a $\frac{1}{2}$ in (13 mm) line to be sufficient, but some areas may require a

Above: This colorful display would be kept at its best with an automatic watering system.
Left: An adjustable dripper on an automatic watering system.

³/₄ in (20 mm) line. Many fittings are available that allow the piping to be run continuously back and forth or around corners according to requirements.

Once the pipe is installed and fastened firmly to the benches or overhead structure, smaller-diameter piping is then run from it into each container or basket, with a dripper attached. For a small area, this alone may be adequate, although, even on short runs, I find adjustable drippers useful, so that containers of differing sizes can receive the correct amount according to their capacity. With long distances, compensating drippers will allow all the containers in the line to receive the same amount of water whether they are first or last on the line.

CHAPTER 11

Propagation

In plants in the natural world, the act of reproduction is through the transfer of pollen from the stamens of the male flower to the pistils of the female, either by wind or insects. This results in the fertilization of the female ovaries and eventually the formation of seed. When ripe, the seedpod splits, allowing the seed to disperse, some of which germinates, thus perpetuating the species.

In the world of horticulture, the natural process can be controlled by using selected plants to obtain seed, which is known as hybridization (see next chapter). In addition, various methods of taking and rooting vegetative cutting material to increase stock are available.

Raising begonias from seed

If the seedlings are to flower in the following summer, the seed must be sown in mid-winter; therefore, it is necessary to have both bottom heat and light. You can, however, raise begonias from seed sown later in the winter or early in the spring, when a warm situation will promote germination just as well. Although there is little chance of seeing flowers that year, the plants will produce tubers by winter, which may be grown the following season. Regardless of timing, the advice is essentially the same.

Preparation

The main key to successful seed-raising is hygiene. The trays should be sterilized before use with a bleach solution. Using the bleach at the rate of one

part bleach to ten parts of clean, cold water, soak the equipment for 10 to 15 minutes, and leave it to drain and dry before use.

The mix required for successful germination of begonia seeds should be fine and have little or no added fertilizer. A name brand is satisfactory, but as an alternative I often put some of my potting mix through a fine mesh and use this. Whichever I use, I mix in about 40 percent of fine pumice or washed river sand for drainage.

It is also advisable to sterilize the mix. "Cooking" the mix in a microwave (six minutes for about 3 to 4 pints (2 L) on a high setting) achieves this. Then wrap the container in a towel and allow it to cool slowly. Alternatively, pour boiling water over the mix and allow it to drain through holes in the bottom of the container. Cool before use.

Regardless of the size of the seed tray, the depth of the mix need not be great. A layer of previously sterilized, coarser material (either pumice, sand or coarse potting mix) about 1.5 in (4 cm) deep placed in the bottom of the tray will assist with drainage. The damp, sterilized, seed-raising mix is then spread over this to a depth of 1 in (2–3 cm) and pressed down lightly with a block of wood to make a flat surface.

Then set the tray in a container of water. To further prevent infection by mold or fungi, use water that is either distilled or previously boiled and cooled, with a small amount of antifungal spray added (mixed according to instructions on the container). Allow the tray to draw up moisture until the surface of the mix is thoroughly damp, then leave it to drain.

Opposite: *Begonia* 'Fred Martin'

Sowing the seed

Now sprinkle the seed evenly over the surface. Begonia seed is exceptionally fine, so the addition of a teaspoon (5 ml) of very fine sand or, failing that, powder sugar to the seed will show exactly where it is falling in the tray, thus ensuring an even spread.

Immediately after sowing, mist the surface using the above antifungal solution so that the seed is wet. Do not overdo this, or the tiny seed may float and fall into the spaces at the edges. At this point label and date the tray—do not rely on memory.

Cover the tray with a sheet of clear glass or place it inside a plastic bag. Then, if it is winter, place it on the source of bottom heat with the thermostat set to keep the mix at a constant 70°F (21°C).

If the seed is sown in springtime when bottom heat is not needed, place the tray in a warm location, though not in direct sunlight, where it will have a temperature range between 65–71°F (18–22°C).

Germination

Germination normally occurs in seven to ten days. Keep the seed damp during this period with misting every four to five days. Turn the glass over each day

Most of these plants and some of the baskets have been raised from seed planted in mid-winter.

to keep large drops of condensation from swamping the tiny seed and, later on, the seedlings. If no germination is noticed after 14 days, try a fraction more heat, but no more than 75°F (24°C) or the seed will cook. Germination will be slower when the seed is planted in spring with no bottom heat and some species seed may take 21 days or longer to germinate.

The tiny seedlings are very susceptible to drafts, so keep the glass or plastic on until the first two leaves show. Then the cover can be moved, allowing a small gap of about ¹/₂ in (1 cm) to give some ventilation. When the third leaf (the first true leaf) is about ¹/₂ in (1 cm) in diameter, the glass can be removed. The seedlings should then be misted daily. Each week, foliar feed with a high-phosphate fertilizer at one-quarter strength to help encourage root growth.

There is some debate over whether begonia seed initially needs light to germinate. Some growers cover the glass with a sheet of newspaper for the first week after sowing, while others leave it uncovered to allow light in. In fact, germination seems to be the same with both methods. However, algae thrive in light, so covering the seeds for the first seven to ten days (until germination) can help minimize algal growth.

Following germination, light is definitely a must. Failure to give young seedlings sufficient light will cause them to go dormant and form tiny tubers. Growth is halted and difficult to get under way again. Begonias, like many plants, are controlled by the number of daylight hours, and 14 to 16 hours are required for natural growth. At an unnatural time, such as mid-winter, supplementary lighting will be needed.

Although any good light source is fine, fluorescent tubes are more economical, and the rectangular light cast is better suited to seed tray shapes than the circle from an incandescent lightbulb. In addition, the fluorescent tubes are cooler and can be placed as close as 3–4 in (8–10 cm) above the seedlings. Normal cool-white tubes purchased from any hardware store are adequate, but better results can be obtained by using wider-spectrum, fluorescent light tubes, such as "Verilux" or "Grolight". This type of tube issues a light spectrum close to natural sunlight and is therefore a big improvement on the normal white-light tubes mentioned above. Although considerably more expensive, they are guaranteed for three years or 26,000 hours of use.

Damping off

Damping off is a fungal problem that can occur with small seedlings, causing them to wilt and die. With a sterilized mix, the nasty pathogens that cause such outbreaks should have all been killed off. As the seedlings start to mature, some ventilation will help prevent damping off.

Sometimes a gray or green mold appears on the surface of the mix. In this case, try increasing the strength of the spray mixtures, and consider also pricking out the seedlings to a new, clean mix, providing they are large enough when the problem occurs.

Transplanting

As a rule of thumb, the seedlings can be safely transplanted or pricked out at any time following the appearance of the first true leaf; the actual timing comes down to personal preference. However, if the tray is crowded, a move is often beneficial much sooner than this. If not, they can be left to grow a little bigger. Continue feeding with one-quarter strength high-phosphate fertilizer.

I generally transplant for the first time into a mix that is halfway in coarseness between the seed-raising mix and normal potting mix, using either flat or segmented trays. The latter have the advantage of little or no root disturbance at the next move, minimizing any setback for the plants.

Sources of seed

Widely available from seed merchants are Semperflorens, Non-stops, and some types of Large-flowered tuberous begonias, e.g., those known as the Memory strain (a group of similar type and mixed colors, but NOT to be confused with individually named begonias), frilled Fimbriata types (Carnation begonias), and unnamed Pendulas or basket begonias. Seed for many species begonias and species hybrids is often available only through societies and special interest groups, many of whom run seed banks for interested growers. Of course, your own efforts at hybridizing are another potential seed source.

Vegetative reproduction

Vegetative propagation of non-tuberous varieties has been covered in an earlier chapter (see page 20), included with each variety description. The following describes methods used for tuberous begonias.

Tuber division

Old books on begonias talk of tuber division as a means of increasing stock, and I still occasionally find it mentioned in gardening columns and programs. Some people cut their tubers up because they think they have grown too large, or that such a method will rejuvenate the tuber.

In fact, the cut tuber sections are still the same age as the old tuber, so the idea of rejuvenation is a fallacy. If a large, old tuber is cut in half, you will then have two old tubers. Furthermore, since roots will NOT grow on any cut tuber surface, the plants derived from this method are likely to be somewhat inferior due to a reduced capacity to take up nutrients. A plant's root system is like the engine of a car—the larger it is, the more power it develops; likewise, the larger the root system, the better the plant that will grow, giving bigger flowers. In addition, there is the increased likelihood of disease affecting the cut surfaces. So this is not a method to be recommended unless as a desperate last resort.

However, having said that, tubers can occasionally be divided. Basket varieties sometimes form a little chain of small tubers joined by a narrow stem. These can be broken off and grown separately. In addition, some upright varieties have tubers that look like a figure eight—in fact, two tubers joined just by a small neck. These can simply be broken off and the resulting small wound dusted with sulfur after trimming. In these instances, there really are two for the price of one.

Propagation by cuttings

The only way to obtain new, vigorous stock is by taking cuttings, which will lead to the production of new, healthy, vigorous tubers. The plants from cuttings should not be allowed to flower in the first season. Remove any flower buds and the growing tip when the plant is 8–10 in (20–25 cm) tall, thus making sure the growth goes into forming a tuber.

Basal cuttings

In my opinion, the best form of cutting material, and the most successful, are basal shoots. As the tubers start into growth in spring, they will often show many buds. Not all of these will necessarily produce shoots, nevertheless, there are usually an excess number of shoots relative to the number of stems desirable on the plant. These shoots can be removed as basal cuttings when they are 3–4 in (7.5–10 cm) in height.

There are two methods of taking basal cuttings, and both are easier if timed to coincide with repotting. The first, which I consider the best, is to clean

Below left: A basal shoot ready for removal.
Below right: A cutting taken, labeled and ready to be put in a propagator.

away some potting mix from the base of the selected shoot, then gently grasp it between finger and thumb close to its base, and rock it to and fro. After a few waggles, the shoot will break away from the tuber. This can be repeated according to the number to be removed.

On all cuttings there will be bracts that protect the dormant buds. Removing these at this point will reduce the chance of their rotting and transferring this rot to the cutting itself. If the tuber has been well-covered with mix, there are also often roots already formed at the base of the cutting, which will give it a head start in life. Place the cutting in a small, clean container and label immediately, giving details of name and the date taken. The wound(s) on the tuber should then be dusted with sulfur or some other fungicide powder. DO NOT dust the cutting itself.

The cutting does not have to be potted up or placed in a propagator immediately. If left for 30 to 60 minutes, the wound at the base of the stem will dry and begin to form a callus over the wound.

The alternative, and probably the most popular, method of removal of the basal shoots is to use a knife or scalpel. This should be cleaned before use

An amateur grower bred this red hybrid.

by dipping it in methylated spirits, then dried with a tissue. At the base of a basal shoot is an eye or embryonic bud. The cut should be made immediately below this eye, which has to be present for the eventual tuber to start into growth the following spring.

The surface of the tuber will have many dormant buds that will form shoots in the years to come. Care should be taken to avoid slicing away part of the tuber when cutting off a basal shoot, for this will destroy some of these buds and impair the productivity of the tuber in future years.

Once the cutting is removed, treat the wound on the tuber as mentioned above. Do not replace the potting mix over the wound, and do not water until the wound on the tuber has dried properly, usually about two days.

Stem cuttings

Stem cuttings, which are obtained by removing a side shoot from the main stem of the plant, are the next best type of cutting. The first four leaves on the main stem will usually develop side shoots. Above

Taking a stem cutting (from left): the first cut, vertically downward, parallel to the main stem; the second cut, sliding the blade along the leaf stem; the "eye" on the finished cutting; the wound on the stem dusted with sulfur to prevent infection.

this on the stalk, the buds are usually flower buds that are of no use as cuttings. It is usual to leave two side shoots to develop fully, to give a really full complement of flowers on the plant. However, if cutting material is in short supply for a particular variety, then the use of these shoots becomes necessary. Not all begonia varieties give these shoots in any quantity. Removing them can at times be difficult because of the restriction of space.

The shoots are removed with a sterile scalpel or small knife by making two cuts, one vertically downward parallel to the main stem, the other below the cutting, sliding the blade along the leaf stem, ensuring that the eye is taken with the cutting. These cuts will result in a wedge shape at the base of the cutting.

An alternative method is to make the cut straight across on the side shoot, just below the first leaf axil, where an eye will generally be found. The remaining stump of side-shoot stem should be trimmed back to about ¹/₂ in (1 cm), dusted and allowed to drop naturally, which it will do after a few days. There is, of course, still an eye at the base

of this stump, which will develop into another side shoot. This could provide a second cutting or be left to grow and flower in due course, but it would be extremely late in doing so.

After treating the wound on the stem (again, never dust the cutting), label the cutting by recording the name of the variety and the date on a plastic label.

Leaves with a dormant bud

Use can be made of any leaves coming directly from the main stem that have a small eye or bud nestled in the axil with the main stem. These are not true leaf cuttings (see page 85), for, if left, they will develop into sideshoots. Using a sterilized instrument, take a very thin slice of the actual main stem and remove the leaf with the eye intact. Treat as for a stem cutting; remember to dust the wound on the stem of the plant.

Methods of rooting cuttings

When I first started taking cuttings, I routinely used a rooting hormone, but now I find the cuttings root just as well without. Two types of hormone are designed to promote root development on the market; one is a powder and the other a gel. The latter has the advantage of sealing off the whole base of the shoot. A similar rationale is behind another idea, that of dipping the lower 1 in (2.5 cm) of the stem of the cutting in honey. This seals the stem from harmful pathogens, thus preventing fungal infection, and is also said to help promote root growth.

Using a misting unit
The most effective way to root cuttings is to use a misting unit. For anyone who intends to take a reasonable number of cuttings, such a system takes much of the guesswork out of the process and decreases the rate of loss.

Cuttings are effectively small plants, though initially without a root system. In order to survive, all plants, large and small, transpire through their leaves the moisture normally taken up by their roots. Cuttings, because they lack roots, cannot replace this moisture. For this reason, they (and newly transplanted seedlings) will wilt. The high humidity in a misting unit helps keep the cuttings turgid until the formation of roots allows moisture to be taken up.

The success of such a unit relies on the temperature differential between the base and the foliage of the cuttings. The mist helps keep the foliage cool, and the constant spray prevents fungi or bacteria spores getting a foothold and causing disease, while the warmth below encourages the formation of roots. With such a unit there is no need for a cover-

ing of any type, and cuttings will be well-rooted in three to four weeks, when they can be potted up into normal potting mix.

Although commercial units are available, the unit does not need to be complex or expensive and can, like mine, be homemade. Essentials are a water supply and a controlling solenoid valve, of the same power rating as the current-reducing transformer to which it is attached, connected to a sensor that controls the actual mist spray. The preferred bed for such a unit is pumice or washed river sand, which needs to be warm—around 65–68°F (18–20°C). The medium can be heated with either a heat board (readily available and easy to install) or by heat cables, and must be thermostatically controlled.

Rooting without a mister
Without a mister, and with care, it is still possible to increase stock or to renew an aging tuber by growing a cutting.

Fill a container about 5 in (12 cm) in diameter with some normal potting mix. Using a spoon, remove the mix from the center of the container to a depth of 2 in (5 cm) and replace it with pumice or sand. Water the mix well, then make a hole with your finger in the center of the pumice/sand and insert the cutting into it. Press the pumice around the stem of the cutting so it is well supported. This

A leaf axil with bud.

The leaf removed showing the "eye".

method will allow both good drainage and air porosity, essential for good root growth.

Now make a simple propagator by cutting the bottom from a clear plastic soft-drink bottle that is large enough to fit snugly inside the rim of the container when placed over the cutting. If the cutting is large, it may be necessary to trim the leaves by up to a third so they do not touch the inside of the bottle; otherwise, the leaves will rot.

Alternatively, use a clean, clear, plastic bag large enough to envelop the whole container. A thick wire in the shape of a hoop placed in the container will support the bag and help prevent the foliage from touching the inside of the bag.

Now leave the container undisturbed in a well-lit place out of direct sunlight for three to four weeks. After this time, the bottle or bag can be removed and the cutting treated as an individual plant. There will be no need to repot the cutting, as roots, which have developed in the pumice, will grow through and into the mix.

Small, cheap plastic propagators, which are available in various sizes from most nurseries, can also be used. In this case, place the cuttings into small containers, say 2 in (5 cm). I have also seen various other innovative methods used with success, from cheap, clear plastic bins, to old fish tanks with a layer of plastic film draped over the top.

Using sphagnum moss

Another simple method of rooting cuttings is to use sphagnum moss. This can be either milled into fine particles or roughly chopped, or even used as is. It is best to cut it up so that the cutting can be easily removed without damaging the roots. Place the moss in a 5–6 in (12–15 cm) container and water, soaking it well. Using a finger, make holes in the moss close to the edge of the container and insert a cutting into each hole, gently pressing the moss around the base of the cutting. When the container is full, place it in a well-lit spot out of direct sunlight and leave for three to four weeks, watering the moss

Cuttings in chopped sphagnum moss.

should it begin to dry out. After this time, the cuttings will be well-rooted and can be potted into potting mix. There is no need to use a mister or cover with a bottle, as the moist moss supplies enough humidity around the cuttings for them to remain turgid.

Rooting in water

Cuttings that have a stem will root quite well in water, and some growers use only this method. Select a container that is a suitable length for the cutting—small jars are ideal, as are orchid phials or clear plastic film containers. Make sure the container is sterile and preferably use distilled or previously boiled water. Put about 1/2 to 1 in (1–2 cm) of water in the bottom of the container, then place the cutting into this and allow it to lean against the side. Place in a well-lit location but out of direct sunlight. Roots should appear in approximately four to five weeks. Roots formed in water tend to be somewhat more delicate than other roots, so allow them to grow only to 1/2 in (1 cm) long before potting the cutting, and take special care to avoid damaging them.

Roots on a cutting grown in sphagnum moss.

Bottom heat

Whichever method is used to grow the cuttings, remember that some form of bottom heat will speed up the rooting time. As well as the heat pads described in the section on a misting unit, above, a heat source can be made from simple products.

I particularly like the idea, used by some growers, of placing about 6 in (15 cm) of moist horse or other animal manure in the base of a deep box and covering it with a layer of plastic. The cutting containers then simply sit on the plastic. I am told that the gentle heat generated by the manure is as effective as a heat pad in speeding up the rooting time.

Leaf cuttings

Until recently, it was always thought that, unlike leaves taken from Rex or other rhizomatous begonias, leaf cuttings from Large-flowered tuberous begonias did not produce viable tubers. However, this has now been disproved. Although slower and somewhat more difficult than using basal or stem cuttings, this method can be very useful for increasing stock of rare or otherwise difficult varieties. It is particularly useful with Pendula varieties, where it is desirable to retain all the initial shoots to give a greater profusion of flowers.

The method of removal is very simple. Again, use a sterilized instrument and make a clean, straight cut through the leaf stem. It does not matter where this cut is made. New leaves from the lower third of the plant seem to produce better results.

Rooting leaf cuttings

A slightly different approach is required in rooting leaf cuttings. It is better not to insert the leaf stem into the rooting medium but merely hold it firmly against the medium. To do this, pierce the leaf with a fine skewer or kebab stick, preferably one that has been sterilized, and push the skewer down into the pumice or sand so the leaf is supported with the stem's cut surface resting on the medium. After about ten days, a swelling and callus will form at the end of the stem, and eventually roots appear. Following this, individual shoots, sometimes as many as ten, will form around the swelling. These shoots will form individual plantlets. At this stage, the entire growing leaf plus plantlets may be potted, or alternatively, the individual plantlets may be left until large enough and potted separately.

The main drawback with this method of securing the leaf is that rot often sets in around the wound caused by the skewer. To overcome this, holes can be made in the selected leaves about a week in advance of their removal from the plant. This then allows the wound to heal and callus before the cutting is taken. A moist environment is essential to keep damp the medium in contact with the cut surface. Again, a mister is the ideal, but the soft-drink bottle method is also successful.

CHAPTER 12

Creating Your Own Hybrids

Hybridizing begonias need not be a daunting task and can bring much pleasure and satisfaction to the amateur grower. From seed, a hybrid cross will never produce a plant identical to the parents. Tuberhybrida begonias are the result of well over 100 years of breeding and therefore have a large and often undocumented gene pool in their makeup. For the amateur hybridist, this means that creating new varieties is a somewhat hit-and-miss affair—but this is part of the fun. Hybridizing makes it possible to produce some really good plants for the garden, for selling, or just to give away, and perhaps even to find that really good one to keep and grow on in successive seasons. Be aware, however, that the seed is very fine. Many hundreds of seeds result from just one pod, so do not go overboard!

Male and female flowers

Begonias, unlike many other plants, have separate male and female flowers. These grow on the same stem, usually in sets of three—a center male flower flanked by two female flowers. Occasionally, one of the side flowers may in fact also be a male. The female flowers are always single and have a three-sided seedpod immediately behind the petals. Finding the female parent for the cross is therefore rarely a problem (see photograph page 47).

The male flowers in species begonias are also single with a collection of pollen-bearing stamens, so there is a wide range of choice for the male (pollen-bearing) parent. Hybrids, however, particularly those of the Large-flowered tuberous types, have over the years been bred for size and double form, during which time the pollen-bearing stamens

of the males have become petals. Naturally, this poses a problem for the would-be hybridizer, since pollen can be difficult to find.

Finding the pollen

Inferior plants may well display pollen on single or semi-double flowers, but the choice from such inferior stock will not produce a better flower or plant. Fortunately, there are some good varieties that will give pollen, usually in the latter part of the season when flowers tend to get smaller and often distorted. In these cases, the center of the flower is often replaced by one or two pollen-bearing stamens, or by rogue stamens that appear among the petals of the flower. It is also possible to force a supply of pollen by allowing early cuttings to flower and then placing them under stress, such as by keeping them dry and deprived of nutrients. The small plant goes into self-preservation mode and produces a distorted, stamen-bearing flower. Among hanging-basket plants, pollen is generally easier to find when the flowers age and become fully open.

Selecting the parents

Some control can be achieved by giving thought to the characteristics of the parents before making the cross.

The first consideration should be the quality of both plant and flower. Well-shaped plants and flowers with good form should be chosen. The size and type of both also matter. For example, are they tall or short? Do the flower stems hold the flower erect? Are the plants floriferous? Are they multi-branching? The criteria considered will, of course, depend

Top: 'Tessa', a Large-flowered hybrid cross.
Above left: The stamens have become petals in this Large-flowered hybrid.

Above right: Distorted petals late in the season may make pollen easier to find. Here, the male stamens can now be seen in the center of this flower.

on the type of plant involved, be it upright, Pendula or Multiflora. But in general, go for quality.

Color choice is somewhat problematic without information concerning the forbears of each plant. However, there are some general rules. For example, if picotee progeny are desired, it is better to use two picotee parents rather than one plain and one picotee, as this will give a higher percentage of picotees.

One final factor in any breeding program is to aim for disease-resistant plants. Don't even consider using a parent plant that is susceptible to any kind of disease.

Above left: The female stigma, and (right) pollen dust that has fallen on the petals from the male stamens.

Above left: Picking up the pollen with a small brush, and (right) transferring it to the stigma.

How to pollinate

Pollination has a better chance of success if done on a warm day with the temperature in excess of 65°F (18°C). Choose female flowers shortly after they first open, when they are at their most receptive. To check if the pollen is ripe, gently tap the stem just behind the male flower. If any pollen dust falls onto the petals, then it is ready for use. With yellow flowers, pollen can be difficult to see using this method, but a small piece of black card or paper held under the stamens will catch the pollen dust. Use a small, soft-haired, artist's brush, preferably sable. Pick the pollen up on the hairs of the brush and transfer it to the stigma in the center of the female flower. Repeat the process more than once to ensure a good take. It is also good practice to do the same cross again the following day, providing there is sufficient pollen, for a better success rate. The brush should be washed and dried between pollinations of differing varieties, or a number of different brushes used. Methylated spirits is useful for the wash, as it dries very quickly.

An alternative method of transferring the pollen requires no tools or instruments. The male flower carrying the pollen is plucked and all the petals gently removed. It is then taken to the selected female flower and the stamens gently stroked across the stigmas of the female, which have a sticky feel. The pollen will adhere to them and fertilization will take place.

Once the pollen has been transferred, a small label should be tied to the stem of the female flower. It should record the name of the female recipient first, and then that of the pollen parent, plus the date. (For example, 'Fairylight' x 'Billie Langdon' 20.2.01 indicates that 'Fairylight' is the female, 'Billie Langdon' is the male, and the cross was made on 20 February, 2001).

Two hybrids from the author's breeding program: 'Vesuvius' (below) and 'Summer Dawn' (above).

If fertilization is successful, the petals of the female flower will fall in four to five days. At this point it is a good idea to place a tie around the stem of the female flower just behind the seed sac, using heavy thread, then fasten it to another part of the plant. The seed sac needs to remain growing on the plant for a further five to six weeks, during which time it will swell and eventually drop off. The tie will prevent the pod from being lost.

An alternative is to place a clean, small, white paper bag right over the seedpod, tying this to the plant. This will secure the pod and also save any seed that may fall from the pod when it begins to dry and split.

When the pod is collected or removed from the plant after six weeks, it is put in a clean, white paper bag (if not already in place) and placed somewhere dry and warm to dry out thoroughly. Do not place in direct sunlight.

Any seedpods that fall prematurely will not contain as much fertile seed as those that have been on the plant for the full term. Providing the pod has remained attached for about three weeks, however, some germination may be possible.

Cleaning the seed

When dry, the seed will have a certain amount of debris with it from the pod, and should be cleaned. Have a number of sheets of clean white paper available. Empty all the seeds from the bag and/or pod onto a sheet. Using a pair of tweezers, remove the large pieces of rubbish, then crease one end of the paper and incline it gently, tapping it so that the seed rolls onto another clean sheet. Repeat the process three times. The good seed will roll off one sheet onto the other, leaving chaff and other debris behind.

Alternatively, use two clean, dry, white china cups. Empty the pod into the first cup, removing any large pieces as described above. Tip the cup on

Right: The pod prior to final drying, with labels attached.

Above: A paper bag is tied over the fertilized seed pod to prevent any seed being lost.

a 45° angle and roll the seed around. A lot of debris clings to the side of the cup. Tip the loose seed into the second cup, clean the first with a tissue, and repeat the process until no debris adheres.

Store the good seed in a small, white paper envelope or wrapped in kitchen foil, recording on it the details of the cross as shown on the label. Place these packets in an airtight, plastic bag or other container and store in the refrigerator until required. Seed will keep for a number of years, although as time goes by, the germination rate will decrease.

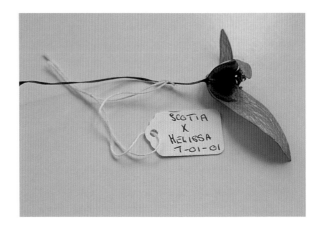

Exhibiting Your Plants

'Bellbridge', a Large-flowered hybrid.

There are many reasons why growers may wish to exhibit their plants or blooms in a flower show, be it a desire to win or just to make up the numbers for a good display. One thing is certain: over many decades, the showing of plants has led to an improved standard in all areas of horticulture.

I have no wish here to delve into the many ins and outs of showing begonias, as there are far too many to mention, especially with the Large-flowered tuberous varieties that require the adoption of special techniques and care for transportation. For those keen to become involved in show competition, I suggest you seek further information from your local society or club or from some of the begonia web sites listed in this book.

Right are some basic general tips that will help pick up extra points.

- Always make sure your entries comply with the show schedule.
- Never exhibit a diseased plant.
- Remove any damaged or marked leaves and other debris.
- Remove any flowers that are past their best, e.g., brown edges.
- Ensure your plant is well-staked and tied where applicable.
- Support the flowers so they look the judge in the eye.
- Top-dress each container with fresh mix.
- Label your plant correctly.
- Water your plant well before the show.
- Make sure each container is spotlessly clean and preferably new.

Useful Addresses

The following is a list of suppliers that I am aware of at the time of writing. In addition to these, most of the societies listed are also sources of supply, and it is through these that rarer collectors' items may be sourced. Most of these suppliers offer online catalogs and ordering. The importation of live plants and plant material across borders requires special arrangements, which will be detailed in suppliers' catalogs.

American regulations vary according to the country of origin and type of plant. Every order requires a phytosanitary certificate and may require a CITES (Convention on International Trade in Endangered Species of Wild Fauna and Flora) certificate. For more information contact:
USDA-APHIS-PPQ
Permit Unit
4700 River Road, Unit 136
Riverdale, Maryland 20727-1236
Tel: (301) 734-8645
Fax: (301) 734-5786
Website: www.aphis.udsda.gov

Canadians importing plant material must pay a fee and complete an "application for permit to import."
Contact:
Plant Health and Production Division
Canadian Food Inspection Agency
2nd Floor West, Permit Office
59 Camelot Drive
Nepean, Ontario K1A 0Y9
Tel: (613) 225-2342
Fax: (613) 228-6605
Website: www.cfia-agr.ca

American Begonia Society
157 Monument
Rio Dell, California 95562-1617
Website: www.begonias.org
E-mail: ingles@humboldt1.com

Antonelli Brothers Begonia Gardens
2545 Capitola Road
Santa Cruz, California 95062
Tel: (831) 475-5222
Toll-free Tel: (888) 423-4664
Website: www.antnelli.com
www.infopoint.com/sc/market/flowers/antonelli
Wide selection including award-winning tuberous bulbs and seed.

Blackmore and Langdon Ltd.
Pensford
Bristol BS39 4JL, UK
Tel: 011 44 127 5332300
Fax: 011 44 127 5331207
Website: www.Blackmore-Langdon.com
Internationally-renowned grower of begonias. Catalog available.

W. Atlee Burpee & Co
300 Park Avenue
Warminster, Pennsylvania 18974
Toll-free Tel: (800) 333-5808
Toll-free Fax: (800) 487-5530
Website: www.burpee.com
Sells the "San" and "Santa" series, and picotees.

Canadian Begonia Society
190 Julia Crescent
Orillia, Ontario L3V 7W9
Website: www.geocities.com/rainforest/4369
E-mail: awagg@sympatico.ca

Cloudy Valley Nursery
935 West Isabella Street
Lebanon, Oregon 97355
Tel: (541) 258-7517
Fax: (541) 258-8694
Website: www.begonias.com
Specializes in fine begonias, unusual, rare and hard-to-find
varieties.

Cruickshank's at Indigo
780 Birchmount Road, Unit 16
Scarborough, Ontario M1K 5H4
Toll-free Tel: (800) 665-5605
Fax: (416) 750-8522
Ships to the United States.

Daisy Farm
Dept B.
9995 S.W. 66th Street
Miami, Florida 33173
Tel: (305) 274-9813
Specializes in rhizomatous, cane, rex and miniature begonias.

Exotic Plants By Beth
1560 Sterling Creek Road
Jacksonville, Oregon 97530
Tel: (541) 899-1662
Fax: (541) 899-1328
Website: www.exotic-plant.com
E-mail: dubie@internetcds.com
Features cuttings from rare and unusual begonias.

Gardenimport
P.O. Box 760
Thornhill, Ontario L3T 4A5
Tel: (905) 731-1950
Toll-free Tel: (800) 339-8314
Fax: (905) 881-3499
Website: www.gardenimport.com
E-mail: flower@gardenimport.com
Ships to the United States.

Kartuz Greenhouses
Sunset Island Exotics
1408 Sunset Drive, P.O. Box 790
Vista, California 92085-0790
Tel: (760) 941-3613
Fax: (760) 941-1123
Website: www.members.aol.com/kartuzexotics
E-mail: mikekartuz @aol.com
Specializes in begonias.

Logee's Greenhouses Ltd.
141 North Street
Danielson, Connecticut 06239-1939
Tel: (860) 774-8038
Toll-free Tel: (888) 330-8038
Toll-free Fax: (888) 774-9932
Website: www.logees.com
Wide variety of begonias. Catalog available online and by
mail.

McClure & Zimmerman
108 W. Winnebago Street
Freisland, Wisconsin 53935-0368
Toll-free Tel: (800) 883-6998
Toll-free Fax: (800) 374-6120
Website: www.mzbulb.com
Sells the "San" and "Santa" series.

White Flower Farm
P.O. Box 50
Litchfield, Connecticut 06759-0050
Toll-free Tel: (800) 503-9624
Website: www.whiteflowerfarm.com
A good range of Large-flowered standard tuberous begonias,
and some baskets. They list a selection of Blackmore &
Langdon named varieties, as well as plants by color range,
and a perfumed range.

A number of other societies outside North America
have interesting and useful web pages. These are:

Association of Australian Begonia Societies Inc.
www.vicnet.net.au/~aabs

Canterbury Begonia Society, New Zealand
www.geocities.com/begoniacircle
This page has links to the above sites as well as to other
useful sites. As author, and as Editor of Begonia News*,*
I welcome inquiries about begonias, to: Mr. Mike Stevens,
47 Burnside Crescent, Christchurch 8005, New Zealand.
E-mail: m.i.stevens@xtra.co.nz

Scottish Begonia Society
www.Scottish-Begonia-Society.co.uk

Southern Region, National Begonia Society, England
www.begoniasouthcoast.co.uk

Selected Bibliography

Catterall, E. *Begonias, The Complete Guide*. London: The Crowood Press, 1991

Catterall, E. *Growing Begonias*. London: Christopher Helm/Timber Press, 1984

Haegeman, J. *Tuberous Begonias, Origin and Development*. Germany: Strauss & Cramer, 1979

Langdon, B. *Begonias, The Care and Cultivation of Tuberous Varieties*. London: Cassell, 1989

Thompson, M. L. and E. J. *Begonias, The Complete Reference Guide*. New York: Times Books, 1981

Index